ONE MAN'S LEG

ONE MAN'S LEG

Paul Martin

GREYCORE PRESS

While I have used real names to acknowledge the many wonderful people I have included in this book, I have opted to change the names of a few people who might otherwise be less than pleased to find themselves mentioned.

Book design by *Kathleen Massaro*

Cover photograph of Paul Martin walking by *Michael Dooley*
BACK COVER CREDITS:
Top: Giant Slalom Racing at the Columbia Crest Cup, Winter Park, CO
Photograph by *John Wieland*
Middle: The run of Buffalo Springs Lake Triathlon, Lubbock, TX.
Photograph by *Elizabeth Kreutz*
Bottom: The Hawaiian Ironman finish line.
Photograph by *Kona Photo Arts*

Martin, Paul, 1967-
    One man's leg / Paul Martin.—1st ed.
    p. cm.
    LCCN 2002141134
    ISBN 0-9671851-5-7

    1. Martin, Paul, 1967- 2. Track and field athletes—
Biography. 3. Athletes with disabilities—Biography.
I. Title.

GV697.M28A3 2002   796.42'092
                                    QBI02-200449

For my parents,
Pauline Martin and Robert Martin…
for the gifts they gave me,
many of which they were unaware.

Acknowledgements

Help was essential in the production of this book. (The same can be said for my life.) Help came from family and friends, editors and sponsors. Perhaps most deserving of recognition are my parents, Bob and Pauline Martin. Without them you'd be reading somebody else's story.

I would like to thank Jennifer Sullivan for digesting the salty first draft and noting that I was no more than 20 percent toward the finished product. Leslie Olson, a former housemate, put her red pen to work on a primitive manuscript and also lent an ear. Thanks go to Andy Johnson and Michele Frieswyk—husband and wife—friends and early editors.

Whitney Lynn believed in me enough to sponsor the mission. Joan Schweighardt believed in the story enough to edit and publish it. After providing the first professional edit, Faye Rapoport thought enough of the project to bring it to Joan in the first place—and then to stay on to work with her to publish it.

Thanks to Judge Cecil Williams, who provided the solitude I needed to get started (though he remains ignorant of his critical role).

Thanks to Scott and Amy Lehr for the laptop that accompanied me to the coffee shop (where the first 60,000 words found structure) night after night.

My perpetual gratitude goes forth to Matt Atwood, Ron Williams, Dr. Rob DeStefano and the many others who opened up their wallets, allowing my focus to remain on sport. Props to Phil LeClair, whose acquaintance provided valuable financial sponsorship.

Athletic competition gave me something to write about. The Challenged Athletes Foundation consistently provided sponsorship to keep me competing. Kurt Hamakawa of the William E. Simon Olympic Endowment—without that single check, I might have sunk a long time ago.

Tom Daley, former marketing manager at Brooks Sports, believed in me and kept the running stuff and the funds coming.

And many more...

The fact that this book even exists leaves me tremendously thankful. That people took the time to help nearly blanks me. That people had faith in my unpopular path inspires me to hold a steady rudder. That many well-wishers didn't understand, yet supported, humbles me.

With deep sincerity, I wish to thank each of you who are taking the time to read this.

Below are some of the companies that supplied the product, and in some cases, cash, to equip my athletic mission:

Current Sponsors:
Össur/Flex-Foot (prosthetics)
Brooks Sports
B & L Bike and Sport
Griffen (bikes)
Veltec Sports (distributors of Sidi cycling shoes, Look pedals, and tires)
Vredestein Rudy Project (technically cool eyewear)
Profile (cycling accessories)
Terry (saddles)
Giro (helmets)
Abilities Unlimited (prosthetic shop)
PowerBar

Former Sponsors:
The Joyce Center (prosthetic shop)
Balance Bar
Bauer Hockey
Cannondale
Schwinn
Rossignol

Table of Contents

INTRODUCTION

When I was 25, I survived a terrible car accident that resulted in the amputation of my left leg below the knee. There were words of encouragement from friends and family, but one underlying thought remained: I would be unable to do so many things I previously took for granted. Through vision, optimism and hard work I came to view the accident as a liberating incident; I have learned how to be me. No more living my life by other people's standards—however sincere they might be.

Even before the accident, friends were always telling me that I should write a book about my experiences. My life seemed fairly average to me. I had grown up in a small city in central Massachusetts, a member of a very large extended family of French Canadian ancestry—tough Acadiens from what is now New Brunswick and Northern Maine who fought harsh oppressors and even harsher winters. My father, Bob, was a construction worker; my mother, Pauline, a homemaker. I have two older sisters, Elaine and Patricia. Before meeting my father, Mom gave birth to my half-brother, Michael, who was soon adopted by my mother's own adoptive parents. Until I was nearly six years old I thought Michael was my uncle. When I was between the ages of five and eight, the family moved to Colorado, then Costa Rica, then Canada, then back to Gardner, Massachusetts.

My home life was aggressively and consistently shaken, and at one point I found myself in a foster home. I made it through high school and worked construction for a couple of years before committing to an education and an engineering degree. This may not have been a typical route to adulthood, but it seemed no more dysfunctional than that of the next guy.

Odd, I thought, that friends would suggest putting my life on paper; by my early twenties, I felt like a regular guy living his life. I couldn't understand why people would be interested in my story.

Since the accident, I've had the good fortune to be able to travel around the world representing my country in triathlon, cycling, running and skiing competitions. I have shared the racecourse with the finest able-bodied triathletes in the world. Through athletic competition, against able-bodied and physically challenged individuals alike, I have found sources of income in the form of sponsorships, endorsements, speaking engagements and grants. I have encouraged students to live their lives with a sense of humor, courage and the right attitude. I have counseled patients before and after amputation. And even more people have asked me, "When are you going to write a book?"

Eventually I came to see that I had a story to tell. But every time I considered writing it, one thought would come to mind: *How in the hell do you do that?* It seemed to me that such a task would take an infinite amount of time and would not be particularly fun—not to mention that I had little writing experience. And if I was going to put a book out there with my name on it, I was bent on writing it myself. I would just have to wait for inspiration...or something that would pass for it.

Opportunity came disguised, as it often does. This time it was a Colorado county judge who ordered me to spend five days in jail, the state's mandatory sentence for driving with a suspended license. At the time of the order, I was competing as a member of the U.S. Disabled Ski Team and was scheduled to serve my sentence after the close of the race season. My season ended three weeks early, so I called the jail superintendent to tell her that I wanted to check in right away. *I couldn't wait to go to jail!*

I now had 120 hours of time on my hands. What better opportunity could I have asked for to begin putting my experiences on paper? I sat down and began writing as soon as I received my orange jumpsuit. The result was a rough draft of some of the chapters of the book you now hold in your hands. I soon became wrapped up in the therapeutic value of facing my toughest, as well as my most glorious, experiences, and seeing the beauty in their relationship. The up-to-then unapproachable task of writing a memoir became a passion.

I am sitting, against regulations, on a pillow on a tiny steel bench attached to a tiny steel desk—and like everyone else here, I'm wearing an orange jump suit. I am writing the opening lines of my story...

> P. R. M.
> Grand County Jail
> Hot Sulfur Springs, Colorado
> March, 1999

My Best Interest

By the time I turned 15 I had already developed a knack for getting into trouble, not only with my parents but also with the law.

The dawn of such activity began eight years before, at the age of seven, when my 12-year-old buddy convinced me it would be lots of fun to enter a newly-built log cabin near our home in Boulder, Colorado and completely destroy every wall, window and light fixture in the place. When Dad walked in, to reel me in for dinner, it dawned on me that this would not be permissible conduct. Tragically, for both my parents and me, knowing such behavior was unacceptable became all the more reason for me to do such things.

Dad moved the family around a lot. We started out in the white-bread city of Gardner, Massachusetts. Dad grew up there and my mother moved to Gardner as a child when her family left French-speaking Moncton, New Brunswick, Canada.

When I was five, we headed to Boulder. Things were good—Mom had never been so happy—but, sadly, this period of our lives only lasted a couple of years. Dad was soon bitten by another traveling bug, and his adventurous spirit drove us southward into Central America, with no particular destination. Somehow, he managed to convince my mother that while we kids were still young, they should live a little.

Costa Rica became our new home. Dad was a union pipe fitter and there was a need for skilled labor in San Jose. Within a few months, however, Mom began to miss the conveniences of home and they decided it would be best to head back to the northeast.

We settled for Saint John, New Brunswick, Canada, where Dad once again found a good job-site opportunity. At the closing of my third grade year, before I could memorize all the words to *"Oh, Canada,"* we were back in Gardner. My two older sisters and I were soon attending Our Lady of the Holy Rosary, the same Catholic elementary school our father had attended.

Gardner was, for the most part, a blue collar town. At one time this heavily wooded community in north central Massachusetts employed more furniture manufacturers per capita than any other city in the nation. To commemorate this unique distinction, several giant wooden chairs tower throughout the city. The largest is about 25 feet tall and sits outside Elm Street School; my initials remain carved into it along with hundreds of others. This masterpiece put our humble community into the *Guinness Book of World Records* until an envious Japanese firm built a taller wooden chair.

"The Chair City" offered scant cultural diversity to its 19,000 residents. But it was prime breeding ground for a small-time troublemaker like me. When we weren't playing hockey, my friends and I found plenty of mischief to get into, from soaping windows and raiding gardens to bombing cars with snowballs. Shoplifting and dope smoking eventually became daily events.

One July afternoon in 1983, when I was a high school sophomore, I was spending innocent time at my girlfriend's house when the phone rang. Brigitte Lavoie was in my grade and our relationship consisted primarily of going ice-skating, illicit drinking and acceptable physical contact. I had the nerve to break the law but not to go to second base.

Brian Bouchard and Rob Maillet (both from hard-core French-Canadian families like mine; they learned to speak French before English) called to let me know that they had grabbed the keys to Brian's grandmother's car. The three of us had been scheming for weeks to take Mrs. Bouchard's shiny blue '79 Pontiac Sunbird for a joy ride. The fact that we were all too young to have drivers' licenses was irrelevant. The boys swung by a few minutes later and soon four unlicensed 15-year-olds were tearing their way around northern Worcester County, Massachusetts.

Brian, Rob and I lived in the same neighborhood and attended both Holy Rosary and Gardner High School together. Despite being a grade ahead of Brian and me, Rob was my best friend; I could be found at the

Maillet residence most Friday nights in the late '70s and early '80s.

There were 11 kids in the Maillet family, so there was always something exciting going on at the top of Ash Street. We played our own version of hockey on our hands and knees in the upstairs family room. We used thick '70s combs-with-a-handle for sticks and a donut-rolled sock with electrical tape wrapped around it for a puck. Knees bled. Fights ensued between Rob and his younger brother John in almost every game.

Rob took his turn behind the wheel for about a half hour. Then Brian drove for a while. We were heading west from Fitchburg toward home when Brian passed a car and quickly cut back into the cruising lane just inches from the guy's front bumper, on par with the expected learning curve. The driver's eyes lit up in anger, Brian's with apology. Brigitte and I sat in the back, feeling somewhat less than safe. Then it was my turn to drive.

I had never driven a car, except to back out of the driveway. I had no idea what I was doing.

It was five o'clock in the afternoon and we were heading down Whitney Street, a fairly steep road, into the glaring sun. The road was a straight shot for a quarter of a mile before it bent sharply to the right. With the sun's rays belting right in my face, I focused on adjusting the visor instead of keeping my eyes on the road. By the time I steered my attention back to piloting the vehicle, it was too late to avoid the consequences of my inexperience. I underestimated the time it would take to reach the 90-degree turn at the bottom of the hill; my foot hit the brake just before the car hit the curb. We ploughed over a crumbled 200-year-old stone wall then plunged through some shrubs and a couple of small trees before finally coming to a stop some 25 feet off the pavement.

We all climbed out, ever so thankful to be unharmed, and began strategizing how the hell we were going to get out of this mess. After plotting for all of 10 seconds, our shock got the better of us and we started running down Whitney, alongside the road we were supposed to be driving on. Clearly, if we got away there would be no chance of getting caught.

However, a local had witnessed the debacle, and before long Officer Gymboris was on the scene filling out a report. My first driving experience ended in disgrace as I was cuffed and tossed into the back of the cruiser, crying in front of my girlfriend and, even worse, in front of my buddies. Humiliating. Embarrassing. Terrifying. I wept in the back seat all the way to the station, terrified by the thought of what my father would do.

With my "one phone call" I contacted my mother, who made the half-hour trip from nearby New Hampshire—where she had moved when I was 12—to bail me out of jail. I hoped she would buffer this latest dose of bad news that Dad would have to absorb.

Before Mom had moved away the two of us had enjoyed a very close and loving relationship. When I was little, I often asked her to sing my favorite song. I don't know the name of it, but the chorus was "tell me why my Daddy don't come home." (I cried every single time she sang it.)

But then she'd reached her limit with Dad and moved across the state line. Her departure was the best thing for her at the time. My parents had married when she became pregnant with Elaine and they were never really in love at any point in their partnership. The resulting family was not a matter of preference.

Mom's move followed not only years of unhappiness but also two years of mental illness; she had had a nervous breakdown when I was 10. Obsessive Compulsive Disorder (OCD), in her case a tic (a reoccurring thought), had spurned her illness. When she realized that there was a problem in 1977, the disorder was not yet understood and effective treatments were difficult to find. In an attempt to erase negative experiences that may have disrupted her sense of well-being, the team of doctors prescribed electric shock treatment, a practice that makes life more complicated for some individuals yet helps others.

Electrodes were placed on specific areas of her brain to zap away memory. What resulted for Mom was little memory of the time surrounding her treatment, a lower IQ and nothing more. No progress, more tics. (A change of hospitals with proper medication and counseling helped get her back on track, and today she is self-reliant and assured. She's independent, and recently bought her own place without anyone's help. This was about the same time she was diagnosed with, and overcame, breast cancer.)

When Mom arrived at the city jail she was as upset as I'd ever seen her. Despite her disappointment, even in her harshest moments, she remained harmless in every sense, compared to Dad. Her big heart and 5'2" stature simply didn't leave room for a mean streak. Mom brought me back to Dad's house where I sat shaking at the dining room table, fear and anxiety pent up inside. Then she searched for the man who would administer the punishment. She found him at the men's club he liked to frequent on the weekend, the same men's club where he had fed me quarters to play Sunday afternoon pinball when I was small.

My father, Bob Martin, was a force not to be taken lightly by anyone. His six-foot frame supported a 230-pound solid mass of flesh. Dark hair, clenched teeth and an unnerving glare rendered him a formidable intimidator, particularly to my 5'6", 130-pound physically underdeveloped self. His demeanor was so frightening to me as a child that I once beat myself up to avoid his rage.

I had a paper route at the time to earn pin money. Much of this money was used to feed the mindless machines at the center of many a young boy's universe—video games. Dad knew my earnings were being endlessly fed to these evil entities: Asteroids, Pac Man and Space Invaders. One day, while we were riding together in his pickup, he questioned me about my spendthrift ways and, too nervous to lie, I fessed up: despite previous warnings, I was still stuffing my money into those boxes. "If I catch you playing those damn things again," he said with teeth clenched and right hand tightly gripped behind my head, "I'll break your fucking neck!"

Dad was not a child abuser in the classic sense; he wasn't constantly beating the snot out of me. He administered the fear factor, often accompanied by a smack upside the head. Too many smacks, in my humble opinion, but the humility always hurt more than the actual smack itself.

He would keep me down, but he would not break my fucking neck.

I wasn't much for learning back then. I continued to plunder not only my earnings but also the money due to the newspaper publisher, which I collected weekly from my customers. I spent all the cash I collected in a three-week period. I was in trouble and I knew it. So I planned ahead.

In front of the mirror that hung on Dad's bedroom door, I stood solemnly with a hockey puck in my right hand, breathing deeply—very, very deeply. First half speed…then harder…more forceful…in the mouth…in the eye. I struck myself over and over until both lips were swollen and my right eye was black and blue. I nervously walked through our back yard, through another yard, then across the street into the back yard of another house, a paper route customer's house. The old lady who lived there was kind, sweet and loving. I knew she would swallow my story. I lay down in her back yard and began to wail. I was so sad that it had come to this that I actually cried honest tears. She came to my assistance with sympathy. "What happened, my dear?" she asked, frowning.

"I…I got mugged. They took all my paper route money." The facial bruises and tears made for quite a believable tale.

Dad called my bluff, but he didn't push the issue. Maybe he had believed me, or maybe he was afraid to see how far his wrath had pushed me.

But there was no self-beating or other action I could contrive to avert his reaction to the car crash. It was time to face the man.

When he came through the door, keen to the situation, my world turned a shade or two darker than it had been for quite some time. He had been drinking, and he was furious. The fact that I had been in trouble with the law on several recent occasions fueled his anger. Shoplifting and beer drinking were already on the list. This case sent him over the edge. After a verbal lashing, he ordered me to my room so he could discuss the details with Mom. Minutes later he burst in demanding to know how I could possibly be so stupid.

"What the hell were you thinking?!" he kept saying over and over and over. He backhanded me a few times. The first backed and buckled me onto the bed, my weight supported by my hands behind me. He bellowed the expected rhetorical questions to which my only answer was, "I'm sorry!" He continued to smack me with an open hand.

In his fury he punched the wall so hard that he split his skin across one knuckle. He had connected with a stud behind the wallboard. I cowered on the bed, propped up on my elbows, head drawn back, peering frightfully toward him.

He stood over me and continued to deliver the open-handed punishment. The broken skin on his right hand was bleeding and he began intentionally flicking blood at my face. Then he picked up the rolling hospital desk I used for homework (on the rare occasions when I did it) and tossed it in the direction of the pine closet he had built in the corner of the room. One hinge busted as the door jam splintered. A caster wheel bounced back at him. I was terrified he would really inflict some serious damage on me before the ordeal would run its course. *What would he do to me next?* I could barely speak.

I sobbed…and felt the hatred slowly building.

He continued to stand above me, flicking, hollering, demanding to know how I could be such "a little asshole." Mom popped in the room and saw Dad's blood on my face and thought it was mine. (Unbeknownst to me, she held this belief for the next 14 years before I could straighten things out.) "You touch him one more time, mother fucker, and you'll find yourself in court!" she said. The heat began to subside after that and I sensed that my life would continue after all.

The next day I told Dad that I wanted to go live with Mom. I simply couldn't stand the thought of remaining in the house with a man who seemingly had no love or understanding for me. I did not tell him I felt this way, but he shot the idea down anyway.

My sister Elaine had similar feelings toward him. She ran away to California at the age of 15 and we didn't see her for another four years. She called on occasion to let us know she was still above ground. Back when I was 10 and Mom's mental illness had left her hospitalized, Elaine had taken over her responsibilities: cooking, laundry, cleaning, etc. This was too much to heap onto a 13-year-old already having a full-blown identity crisis. Elaine grew up quickly in every sense. Her physical features developed early, as did her curiosity for adult behavior. It was around this time, when she was 13, that she had her first drink at the bar. Dad heard about that one and, flashing a photo of her, told the barkeep that if he ever let her in there again he would deeply, deeply regret it.

On the contrary, Paty (that's how she spells it) still lived with Dad and me and held my father's respect. She was president of her high school class for three years, had earned five varsity letters in various sports and was enrolled in the University of New Hampshire for the upcoming year. Despite having the same upbringing as Elaine and me, she took a different approach. She considered Mom to be weak and didn't respect her because of her inability to be a force in the home.

Eventually Dad had a change of heart on the matter of my living with Mom. He indignantly told me to go ahead and move out. If I thought living with her would be beneficial to me, he said, then I should go ahead "and keep running from reality." Ironically, I did feel as though I was running from reality—running to a safer, more loving place. I was well aware that I was not the ideal son, but I knew a more nurturing home environment could help remove some of the daily resentment and conflict. I was undoubtedly too scared of, and disillusioned with, my father to discuss possible ways to improve our relationship. I felt his standpoint would be "stop getting into trouble!" My solution was to buck the system and see how much I could get away with.

I was trying to win the battle. He had laid down the ground rules, which, of course, I found bothersome. To ensure I followed these rules, he instilled the fear of physical punishment. I thought that the more things I got away with, the braver I must be. Continually testing the limits by breaking the law—his law—meant I was an exceptionally brave young man; fear of consequences might deter most individuals from shady behavior, but not me.

To me, my father was the bravest, strongest and worldliest man on the planet. In many ways I wanted to grow up to be just like him. I wanted to be respected, just like him. Trying to match the man was a big part of the problem.

Before she'd left my father, Mom and I had decided that I would go to live with her when she settled down. When she first came for me a few weeks after she'd left, however, I didn't have the guts to leave my high school and my friends for a fresh start in another town. I also feared leaving the financial comfort Dad provided, however humble it was, to struggle with her. But now that this latest situation had arisen, she could not have been more willing to take me into her home. So I moved in with Mom and her new husband.

Her new husband, I soon discovered, was a man short on character. He worked for a local asphalt paving company, had little money and showed my mother little respect. It seemed to me that she needed a man for support and had settled for the first one who gave her the attention she felt she needed. She was "on the rebound," the classic "wrong" time for relationship-hunting.

They lived in a trailer in the countryside and maintained a very modest lifestyle. I lasted about a week there. It was simply too cramped a space for Mom's husband to share with a teenage kid. He didn't much care to have me around and that was tough on Mom. She told me I would have to leave, that it would be in my best interest. I understood. She was doing the best she could do for me at the time. (Mother divorced him just two years later, and he died not long thereafter—by electrocution while trying to steal copper pipe from a condemned building.)

Mom often asked me to divulge my feelings toward her and my father regarding their divorce and her abandonment of her family. I never shared much of my feelings on the subject because I honestly didn't have much to share. My only opinion was that it was nice not to have to listen to the two of them argue. After the divorce, Dad still came home drunk quite often, Paty was still the favorite and Elaine did her best to take over where Mom left off. I continued to play hockey and to get into trouble where and when I could.

I was comfortable with the divorce. I think Paty was also glad to see an end to their futile attempt at compatibility. Elaine felt differently. Mom was her home. Maybe she stayed with Dad after Mom left because I chose to stay with Dad. Maybe she felt a responsibility to take care of me. Maybe she would have preferred to live with Mom. I don't know; I never asked.

When I returned to Gardner, I stayed here and there with friends for a few weeks. School was about to start and I didn't have a home. Damned if I would go back to live my father. I briefly considered moving in with extended family members, but this would mean some sort of tie to him. Mom didn't have many local relatives. If I was going to do this, it would be without any association to him.

A high school friend of mine, Cindy Nelson, told me that her mother, Linda, was a foster parent and suggested I consider living with them. I rejected the idea at first; living as an "orphan" in someone's home held very little appeal. Besides, I'd known Cindy had a crush on me for some time, and while I considered her a friend, I didn't return her interest.

But after a few discussions at the Pleasant House of Pizza, our crew's hangout, Cindy finally convinced me that living with them had potential. She told me that her mom was easy-going and the living situation was not your typical foster home experience. For example, Linda drove a very hip Camaro Z-28. There was no man of the house other than her cousin, Greg, who was in his early twenties and whom I had known from around town. I was desperate for a place to live; the situation began to sound ideal.

I investigated my eligibility a few days later at the Department of Social Services office downtown. I visited without an appointment. It was a nervous visit, checking myself into a foster care system I knew nothing about.

The social worker, Donna, was both informative and cooperative. She was tall, blonde, plainly attractive and genuinely cared about my predicament. We discussed the circumstances that had brought me to her door. She agreed that they constituted a strong case for pursuing a new environment.

A meeting was arranged for Donna, my father and me. But Dad failed to show up, and he failed to show up the next week, too. When he did appear for the third scheduled meeting, his stay was brief. Dad immediately and adamantly argued against any benefit I might gain from being part of the foster care system. He rigidly maintained that I was only running away from my problems. With no intention of hearing Donna's thoughts, he got up and left. His brevity and abruptness prompted Donna to sign the papers at once, placing me in the care of Linda Nelson.

During one of my trips back to the house to gather my things, Dad tried to convince me to join the army. He was afraid I would be bounced around to several homes before I finished high school and that I wouldn't graduate. His concern seemed genuine. He thought, too, that the military might make a man out of me. I was 16 years old. I couldn't fathom the idea of being a soldier.

Cindy and I became like brother and sister, with the usual high school sibling problems. More often than not we had some sort of conflict in the works. *Whose turn is it to do the dishes? What channel are we going to watch? What is taking so long in the bathroom? When are you going to get off the phone?* We still had the same friends and went to most of the same parties. We were brother and sister. (Later Cindy would write to me to express her appreciation and love for me, the nearest thing she'd had to a real brother. It was a touching letter.)

Throughout my first year in the house, I had several foster siblings. Two stood out from the others: Bart, a dirtbag from nearby Winchendon, and Lori, the daughter of a Hell's Angel.

Bart, who was a year younger than me, had been in trouble with the law on several occasions. He was short and somewhat stocky—and he always had a nasty case of B.O. He had been kicked out of his mother's house for, among other things, stealing her cash. He also stole from me—the same day he was kicked out of Linda's house. He'd snagged a pair of Ozzy Osbourne concert tickets meant for Rob and me.

I discovered the details of the missing tickets several days later. Soon after I saw him roaming the streets of Gardner. I was 16, and I was with my friends and thought I had to be tough. It seemed appropriate to rough him up a bit in retaliation. I approached him as he entered a phone booth. I was not really much of a fighter, but I felt I had to be physical to retain my pride. I questioned him about the tickets and, of course, he denied having had a hand in the matter.

I threw a few half-hearted punches, for the sake of the crowd more than anything else. I had wanted to kick his ass, but I discovered it just wasn't in me.

The next day the boys were calling me Muhammad Ali. I chuckled but secretly felt a bit shallow for reaching for approval through violence, even though I hadn't delivered a meaningful blow.

The Hell's Angel's daughter, Lori, was 15, weighed 220 pounds, and didn't last very long either. She and I got along fine. I enjoyed her company when she wasn't trying to impress everyone with her tough talk. Her father had allegedly killed a man to earn his club colors and this made her proud—at least on the outside. When she threatened Linda over a curfew issue, she was ejected.

The middle years of high school were dark years for me. My self-esteem was lacking and my insecurity peaked. I wasn't living with my real family and the future looked bleak. My immediate surroundings were reasonable but I had no idea where I was going. I even passed on the Gardner High hockey team that year. My ability to mind the net for the Wildcats had been the one aspect of my existence that I was truly proud of, because it was about the only thing I felt I could do well. The greatest self worth I felt as a kid was when the hometown crowd would chant my name after I made a particularly impressive save. They weren't chanting, "Go-Paul...Go-Paul...Go-Paul!" They were chanting, "Pooo-pah ...Pooo-pah...Pooo-pah!"

I'll explain: No more than a week out of the womb, I was an over-achieving diaper-messer. My mother termed me a "little pooper" and the nickname followed. Family, friends and coaches referred to me as "Pooper" ever after. With the proper Bostonian accent, it's "Poopah."

And there are variations: Poop (which seems to be the most popular), Poops, Poopy, Poopsy, Pooperman, Crapper, Shitter, etc. You could say the nickname was, for me, the special identity every child searches for.

Ice hockey had helped direct my energies in a positive direction more than anything else back then. I had been the go-to guy as a running back in the Pop Warner football league from ages 10 to 13, but I was too small to star at the high school level. At eighth grade graduation, we lined up short to tall and I was the progression's flagship. I sat the bench as a Gardner High Wildcat sophomore year. Watching the game from the sidelines was too much for me to handle and I quit the team before the close of the season.

My future on the high school ice hockey team had looked solid as early as my freshman year. Maurice "Fitzie" Fitzgerald, the head coach, let me practice with the varsity squad and also allowed me to dress for home games. My smaller-than-average size didn't affect my performance as a goaltender. Players and coaches alike were impressed with my courage and determination. My glove wasn't the fastest nor were my feet the quickest, but I had guts. I was the smallest guy out there, putting myself in front of slap shots I had never seen the likes of before.

But in my junior year, competition suddenly stood between me and the starting position I had coveted since freshman year. Troy Hanks, a sophomore, was new to the team and was undoubtedly better than I was in the net. He was bigger and faster and had better body control. My self-esteem plummeted further still.

Rather than try to compete for ice time, I quit the hockey team in favor of a second part-time job. I had already been working with Rob in a supermarket meat department. Our duties after school included cleaning the entire butcher room and an occasional assignment wrapping meat. I took a second job cleaning floors at a local manufacturing company. Several other buddies worked there from 6 to 9 p.m. When my shift was through at the Food Farm, I would buzz up to Simplex Time Recorder a mile up the road and arrive with little time to spare.

The money I earned went to concert tickets, dope and other random stuff. I didn't save a dime. The once-promising young athlete was now smoking lots of pot and showing little ambition to do much else.

I got busted with the weed while walking home from a party with an empty keg on my shoulder, and I was put on juvenile probation for six months. The punishment was a drag but it paled in comparison to the words I received from my father a few days after the sentencing.

One Saturday morning, as I lay lazily in bed, I heard a knock on the foster home door. I dragged myself out of my room in nothing but my Fruit of the Looms. It was him.

"You gonna quit smoking that shit now?" he aptly questioned.

"Probably not."

"You know what you are, Paul? You're a loser! You're a fucking loser!"

He stammered away. I stood where I was in disbelief. Then I wallowed back to bed. And began to cry…and cry…and cry. I was hurt, not so much by his words, but more by the degradation of our relationship. *How did we grow so far apart? What was at the heart of my slanted behavior?* I really didn't know.

The following year I began to straighten up. It was a slow process; I continued to smoke pot and even played around with cocaine and acid. But I also rejoined the hockey team. And somehow, in the midst of it all, I was voted runner-up for homecoming king.

In physics class, by far the most challenging class of my pre-college education, I managed to amaze some of the more intellectual kids. I had a grasp on the concepts and consistently scored well on tests. But what really amazed them was that physics was first period, three days a week, and it was well known that I was freshly stoned in the morning. Some of them questioned how it was that I could possibly have an understanding of the course material with my altered state of mind. I answered, "Well, later on in study hall I understand it."

I began to see that I wasn't totally without hope. I just needed someone, a mentor, to provide a little direction. Howard Sherman, a psychologist in Boston, surfaced at just the right time. A friend of mine had been visiting him and suggested I do the same. Howie knew I wasn't in a position to pay and agreed to help me for free.

I looked forward to getting on the train to Boston. There was something adventurous about a trip to the city. My small town held no secrets; Boston symbolized the possibilities of discovery. My good friend, Al St. Pierre, began to come with me to seek Howie's guidance. The city trips were even more enjoyable with him.

I enjoyed the time Howie and I spent together. He did, too. He listened, and he understood. I felt no shame and no need to withhold my deepest emotions when we talked. I told him about my big ambitions— not that I had any in particular, but I did believe I might be somehow special. Although I often felt like I was the least interesting person in the room, I believed that if people would only take the time to talk to me, they'd find something special in me, and help me find it, too.

Despite my lack of confidence, I believed I would succeed at something. The question was, at what?

Howie urged me to consider college. Not only did he convince me that an education was an experience I didn't want to miss, but he paid my application fees out of his own pocket! He paid for six in total, all of them to state schools. As a ward of the state, I had the opportunity to attend any of these institutions that would accept me with waived tuition and room and board fees.

Here was a realization: negative experiences, like being a foster child, could provide tremendous opportunity. Per Howie's advice, I applied to these colleges as an undeclared Liberal Arts major to leave myself open to fields that might interest me as my education progressed.

Within two months, I received letters of rejection from the University of Massachusetts, Salem State College, and Westfield State College. I had thought my combined score of 1150 on the SAT would be sufficient to get me into any state school. Then the letter came from the University of Lowell, in Lowell, Massachusetts. They had accepted my application! They were offering me an education! For the first time in as long as I could remember there was a specific, bright path to pursue.

Hockey season was great that year. Troy had joined an AAA team, which left me an opportunity to play again. Fitzie was not pleased with the trouble I was still getting into, or that I had blown off the prior season, so I had to fight for the starting spot. A junior year prospect, clearly less talented than I, was a good kid with a desire to try. He received the nod as the starting goaltender.

I was disappointed but understood the reasoning. I would have to be patient and wait for my time to come. We lost four of the first six games before I was given a chance to prove myself once again.

Fitzie started me in the net against a mediocre team. I registered a perfect game; no goals were scored against me. A shutout. I registered two more shutouts in the next several games. Jay Gearan, an English teacher, reported high school sports for *The Gardner News* and continually touted the team's latest success.

The season continued to go well and we qualified for the Division II State Championship Playoffs, as we had every year. We out-scored our first two opponents and went on to the quarterfinals to face Oxford High. There were seven and a half minutes left in the third period with the score tied 2-2 when a broken stick was left floating behind my net. After the whistle blew at the other end of the ice, I grabbed the pieces and tossed them over the glass behind me. There were no people or seats or anything else there that would have deemed this an irresponsible action; I was simply removing the stick from the ice. It was, nonetheless, a big mistake.

Throwing anything over the glass, it turned out, constitutes a major penalty. It's a safety issue. The penalty time for a major is half a period, or seven and a half minutes; hence, my ice time came to a premature end. The second stringer was out with the flu. Our third string freshman was about to play the biggest game of his short career. We lost 4-3.

I ended the season with three shutouts, tying the Wildcat record.

In the meantime, Linda Nelson's mom had become very ill and Linda had gone to stay with her. Cindy and I had, in effect, no supervision for my entire senior year. What luck! (All due respect to Linda's mother.) Naturally, Cindy and I did have a few parties but nothing as out of control as one might expect. Donna, the social worker at DSS, was none the wiser.

A car crash had led to my entrance into the foster home and another crash ended it.

My transportation in those days was a Takara 12-speed road bike. One day, a light rain had begun to fall on my ride home, when I was less than a mile from the house. I picked up the pace a bit in an effort to stay dry. I smiled and waved hello to a friend working at a gas station on the way. Moments later a van towing a trailer pulled onto the street from the right, about a hundred feet in front of me. I was spooked for a moment, until I realized the tandem was at a safe distance. Just as my way cleared, a station wagon, whose view of me had been blocked by the van and trailer, crossed the street from the left to enter the street that the van had exited.

My eyes met the old man's eyes and my front wheel met his right fender. My eyes remained fixed on his as my head and elbow hit the windshield. Then flesh met pavement some 20 feet on the opposite side of the vehicle. I stood up in protest only to fall back down just as fast. My back and my right leg were both in unbearable pain.

Witnesses helped me to an adjacent knee-high wall. A good friend, Kevin Dech, happened to be passing by and came over to view the carnage. When Kevin recognized me he exclaimed, "Poop, your arm is hamburg!"

The elbow that met the windshield received multiple lacerations and glass remained embedded in my arm. The emergency room nurse offered her sympathy as she cleaned the wounds. I moaned and groaned as the shards were systematically scraped from my flesh.

My left arm would bear scars, but no tendon or bone damage. The back pain was the result of muscle spasms and my left leg received a deep bruise and lost a little skin. My right ring finger broke at mid-digit and received a dozen sutures. (Two years later, after legal fees, I would be paid $4,500 in settlement; I thought I'd won the lottery!)

While in the ER getting stitched, I saw a friend of my father's who had just left the club—for whatever reason—and was heading back. He mentioned seeing Dad there earlier and that he would let him know of my mishap if he was still there. Sure enough, a half hour later Dad came into the emergency room, smiling. He had been informed that I was fine and there was little to worry about. I was glad to see him and in a jovial mood despite the damage. I was joking with the medical team when he arrived.

This accident had occurred a couple of weeks after my high school graduation, which brought all our immediate family members together. By then we had all come to understand one another with increased compassion. For the first time in years, I found I was not afraid of my father, a huge step in reestablishing a friendship. My mother had left her husband by then and had settled into one of the apartment houses Dad owned. My sister Elaine had come home after several years on her own. And Paty and I had opened channels of communication that had previously been closed. The animosity that once stood between any two of us seemed a thing of the past. Dad even bought Mom a little red sports car.

Who Am I?

I moved into Bourgeois Hall dormitory at the University of Lowell in the fall of 1985. Two friends helped carry my paltry possessions to their new environment. I hadn't told my family that I was heading off to college. I knew my father would find out, but it was going to have to be through the grapevine and not because I'd told him.

We were all on good terms now, and any one of my family members would have wanted to know, but we didn't particularly think of one another as good friends. The exception was Mom and Elaine, who had become tight after Elaine returned from her four-year soul-searching excursion. I was still struggling to establish my independence, so calling any of them for help or blessings was not something I was prepared to do. A part of me was sad that they weren't there to share in the move, that they weren't there to witness the beginnings of what I believed would be a prosperous future.

It was a great day nonetheless, moving into the dorms with four years of unrestricted enlightenment ahead of me. There was fun to be had, a potential girlfriend to meet, a future to develop. At some point before high school graduation, I had decided on a career as an airline pilot. Chicks would dig an airline pilot. I could brag about emergency landings, worldly adventures, a new Corvette and Harley-Davidson—and my parents would be proud of me. My class picture had been pasted in the college-bound section of *The Gardner News* with "Aeronautical Science" underneath it in bold print. I didn't even know if that was a major at *any* university, but it sounded impressive and legitimate. In an effort to take a strong step in the right direction, I joined ULowell's Air Force Reserve Officer Training Corps.

Within the first few days of my participation in the ROTC, I was exposed to enough military zealots to completely lose interest in the program. The pock-marked senior officer-in-training who commanded our freshman group of young Air Force hopefuls harped on me for wearing a wrinkled T-shirt to class early in the week (we had not yet received our uniforms). That pushed my already unstable buttons and I snapped at him, making it clear that my interest had expired. My ROTC career was over almost before it began.

I was chasing a dream by joining the ROTC. Reasonable enough. The problem lay in the fact that I wasn't ready—not for that dream, anyway. Had I been ready, I would have questioned authority long before rejecting it.

Besides flying planes, I had another collegiate dream to chase—a distant one, but it had some potential. I wanted to play ice hockey for a Division I school. I hoped to earn a spot as a "walk-on" to ULowell's NCAA program. The Hockey East Conference to which our school belonged hosted some of the best college hockey in the country. This conference included the likes of Boston College, Boston University, University of New Hampshire, Harvard, University of Maine, Northeastern and Providence College. This was big time hockey.

One of my teammates from the Gardner High hockey squad, who was also enrolled at ULowell, told me I wouldn't make the cut. Growing up I was good enough to play any sport I had a genuine interest in, so I was never told "you won't make the team." I never had to worry about it. In this case I had to stop and think about it. Was I wasting my time? Would I humiliate myself? I knew I wasn't NHL material, but I had nothing to lose. I was starting to think big and I liked it.

I fought for a spot on the junior varsity squad. I practiced with both the JV and varsity members in dry land training and preseason drills for about a month, starting in late September. There were seven contending goaltenders vying for three available slots on the second tier team. In the coach's opinion two of the stronger, more experienced goalies had poor attitudes. The coach was new to the team and didn't want any leftover baggage, so he canned them both. And then there were five. Coach offered spots to two of the prospects, neither of which was me. The remaining three of us were given a one-time opportunity to make the roster since the coach claimed that he simply couldn't decide who to cut and who to keep. When Boston College came to town for a scrimmage, Coach gave us a period apiece. The least effective net-minders would get their walking papers.

The second period was all mine. *OK, here we go. Time to shine, you're a wall, nothing gets by ya. You made the high school varsity team freshman year. You're a wall.* I would like to repeat that period. I let three shots sneak by in the quick 15-minute test. Game over for me, along with any further hopes of playing Division I hockey.

Thankfully, the academic side of college was going well at least: Political Science, U.S. History, College Writing. Pretty easy stuff if you simply did the reading.

The problem was that, in spite of the good grades, I lacked any interest in the subject matter. What did I care why the Whigs were renamed Republicans or why the Democrats were originally called Republicans? I had always been better in math and science but had chosen Liberal Arts under Howie's guidance.

So there I was with an extremely short-lived career as a pilot, a realization that I had reached the last rung of my hockey ladder, not much interest in my classes, and no true family unit to turn to. I had not developed any strong friendships. I found myself hitchhiking home most weekends to party with the boys.

By November, I called it quits. College life wasn't working for me. I went back to Gardner to live with a few friends I had stayed with earlier in the summer. I tried to get a job driving a cab with my good friend Al St. Pierre, but I couldn't get a hackney license because of the marijuana possession charge from a year ago. I began to miss my family.

In the two and a half years I had spent living elsewhere, my father had managed to relax a bit. The majority of my sour feelings toward him had also dispersed. He had only my sister Paty under his roof now and she was mostly away at school, which made things easier for him. Furthermore, she never caused headaches even when she was at home. Dad was proud of her.

Dad and I had lunch one day. We met at D'Angelo's sub shop. I ordered the usual Philly steak with onions, peppers and cheese. He got the same. That's when I told him I had dropped out of school.

Then it was time. I asked if I could come back home.

In a pleasant, non-condescending manner he said, "Of course you can. Are you willing to live under my rules?"

I nodded.

Dad's disappointment with my decision to quit school so quickly led to a warm heart-to-heart talk. He did his best to impress upon me the importance of an education, encouraging me to take advantage of the opportunity before being lulled into the working world without the means to go back. In the end, he realized that I would not be returning to school in the immediate future. He did get some satisfaction out of knowing I would be working at a "real" job.

Through Gardner's unemployment office, I had already landed a job working construction with The Jaillet Welding Company. I had no prior experience in construction other than helping build a couple of forts as a youngster and helping Dad with his remodeling projects. He owned two previously condemned apartment houses, which he had renovated himself, single-handedly. It was his ability to tackle any construction task that led to the most practical advice he ever passed down to me. One day, when I was just a kid, I asked him how he was able to do all those things. He replied, "I can do it because the other guy can do it." With those words ingrained in my mind, I was confident I could do what would be asked of me.

Peter Jaillet, the company's president and founder, was young, 28, and "a real go getter" according to Dad. Pete patronized the bar my father had recently bought, The South Gardner Hotel. Built in 1799 as a hotel, it had most recently served as a boarding house, a place for transients and those who live a life without frills. It also happened to be the first place in Gardner my grandfather walked into in 1939 when he arrived from New Brunswick, Canada, at the age of 26, unable to speak English and thirsty for a beer.

Pete was often thirsty for beer. His company, a structural steel erection firm, employed beer drinking men. What started out as a guy in welding school progressed into a one-man fabrication shop and then to a half dozen men erecting small structures, and finally to a company of 30 non-union ironworkers erecting eight-story office buildings. Men who do this kind of work drink beer.

Not long before taking the job, I had listened to my friend Brian's hairy "walking the steel" stories; he had been working for Pete for a year. When I took the job, I didn't know it was the same company or even that I was signing up to put my life at risk on a daily basis for $6.50 an hour as an ironworker. I simply thought I was going to learn how to weld stuff. I rode to work on Day One with Brian and another guy…for an hour and a half! I couldn't believe it. Every day? Ninety minutes just to get to work? It seemed like such a waste of time.

The first day on the job was no ordinary one. I was a man among men. Until then every job I had ever held was a means of earning a few bucks to buy beer and pot and concert tickets. Now I was working the kind of job men worked to earn a living. I spent the day with men who expected me to work like a man who works for a living—men who drank on the way home and then got up and did the same thing all over again, day after day. It was a coming of age of sorts.

After less than an hour on the job it was time to walk the steel. Like most others, I couldn't stand and walk at first, not even a mere 12 feet off the ground on the first floor. I took it slowly and began by straddling the I-beams. I scurried around with my feet atop the bottom flange, my hands tightly gripping to the top flange. (An I-beam looks like an "I," the top and bottom lines are the flanges.) This wasn't a bad way to get around—until I was asked to do something.

My first job on the steel was dragging deck. Decking is corrugated sheet steel that constitutes the base of a floor on which concrete is later poured. The lengths run perpendicular to the floor beams or joists. A stack of deck sheeting is placed by crane on the framework of a completed floor. Then individual sheets are spread side by side, interlocking along the outer corrugation, across the beams until the soon-to-be floor is completely covered. An experienced worker will walk either forward or backward along a beam that is perhaps three to four inches wide, dragging one end of a typically 15- to 30-foot sheet while his partner works the other end in the same fashion. The inexperienced worker straddles the beam, which takes considerably longer. The process of going from straddle to walk is greatly expedited by a partner who doesn't enjoy waiting for the rookie to drag his end. By the end of the day, I was walking.

My second day on the job brought another challenge. When I arrived at the job site, I was asked to drive to another job site to pick up a welding machine. Pete gave me the keys to a four-wheel-drive, four-door, manual four-speed Ford Crew Cab and told me to follow him. My only experience driving a manual transmission was at the wheel of my father's little red pickup a couple of years earlier. I had driven it twice.

Once again, I knew damn well that I had no right to be behind the wheel. But I was not about to tell the boss I couldn't do something as simple as drive a truck. Dad's long-ago words came to mind: *I can do it because the other guy can.*

I made it out of the yard, bucking within reason. The road to the other job site, Route 9, was littered with stop lights, forcing me to stop over and over again. I must have stalled the damn truck 20 times on that 20-mile trip. When I got there, Pete asked, "Don't you know how to drive a stick shift?"

"I do now," I replied.

He laughed, maybe appreciating my gall.

At the second job site, a crane lowered a Lincoln Electric SAE 250 gas-powered portable welding machine onto the truck bed. Pete had sent me off to get this 2,000-pound, $5,000 machine—and the $10,000 truck—to their destination.

I bucked my way back to the first job site in Framingham violently. The welding machine slammed back and forth repeatedly because it hadn't been tied down. Had anyone else been driving, there would not have been a need to strap it. At one stoplight a man pulled up next to me with a concerned look on his face and told me that I had lost some cables on the road. I assumed the cables in question were steel ropes, "chokers," which were only a few feet long and not terribly expensive. *Who would miss them?*

"That's cool," I said, trying to look calm.

At the next stoplight a van pulled up next to me and a man got out of the driver's seat, reached back into the van and pulled out a large coil of welding cable. It was probably 50 feet long with a price tag of about $400. He threw it into the bed of the truck with a disgusted look and said, "Here, you dropped something."

"Hmmm…," I wondered. "How in the world did that fall out?"

I finally pulled onto the job site, proud of my accomplishment. My buddy waved back at me as Bruce Jaillet, Pete's older brother and second in command, came screaming.

"What the fuck?! Look at this fuckin' tailgate!"

My bewildered look bespoke my ignorance.

"You don't have a clue, do you? Get out here and take a look!"

I got out, still wondering why he was so pissed off. Then I saw the problem, plain as day. The welder was hanging nearly halfway off the bed of the truck from all that bucking. The only reason it hadn't slid off onto Route 9 was that the tailgate hinges hadn't completely broken off. The tailgate had folded into a nearly 90-degree angle, with the hinges fully extended and pointing inward.

Throughout my two years on the job I learned a lot about myself and a lot about people. About myself: I'm a hard worker. It is important to me to give it my all. I enjoyed impressing my workmates with hard-nosed labor, and my know-how regarding mechanical things began to shine through. About others: don't expect them to share your passions. My ability to work hard under poor conditions, such as rain and snow, stood out after listening to the others complain. I went from a bolt-stuffer to joist-welder and then to connector within a year.

Being a "connector" was one of the most envied jobs on site, other than that of crane operator. A connector and his partner accept pieces (beams, columns, joists, deck stacks, etc.), commonly referred to as pics, from the crane for assembly. They connect the pieces by bolting them together like a big erector set. When I became a connector, eight months or so into the job, I needed Joe, the latest in a series of transient experienced workers, to show me the ropes.

The site was a new apartment building on the waterfront in Hampton Beach, New Hampshire. Construction was already underway when Pete offered me the job. I had become a good climber and looked forward to the position.

My comfort on the iron was obvious, but minutes into this new job I was presented with another experience that would require some nerve. We were on the fifth floor with no decking below us for three stories. Our task was to set the first pic of the sixth floor, which bridged two columns, cantilevering each. Each man sat on his end of the beam while the crane line supported it. Joe gave the signal and the crane operator began to raise the beam toward the tops of the columns. We guided the beam, and ourselves, by placing a hand along the column as we ascended.

Picture this: I'm on a six-inch-wide beam, nine inches deep. There is a three-inch flange on either side of the web where I can place my feet, nine inches below my butt, and I'm 45 feet over the nearest completed floor on a 30-foot teetering beam. On the other end is a man who at any moment could bobble and cause us both to take a dive. Joe had to be thinking that he was in the same predicament as I was, with a rookie on the other end. And of course both of our lives depended on the steady hand of the crane operator.

We reached the necessary height and Joe quickly fastened his end, affording me the comfort of knowing that my end was then infinitely more manageable. I only needed to align the bolt holes via my spud wrench, a 10-inch open-end wrench that tapers to a point on the opposite end to be used for bolt hole alignment. I placed the spud through a hole on the bottom flange of the beam. With my free hand I gave the signal to the crane operator to slowly lower the beam as I matched the corresponding hole atop the column. Using my left foot to manipulate the freestanding column, I rendered the two pieces into alignment. With the beam now supported, and some tension remaining on the cable, I was able to bolt one of the remaining three holes. I was then reasonably safe. Joe walked across the lone, wobbling beam to unhitch the crane while I nervously stuffed another bolt on my end. My heart calmed, my mind cleared and I descended the column so we could do it all over again in the adjacent bay.

Such is the life of a connector: climbing steel, tool belt loaded with 50 pounds of bolts, spuds and a hammer, assembling a new structure. I put on nearly 20 pounds in the first year—20 pounds of muscle. Working for Pete did for me what my father had hoped the army would do.

Now Dad and I had a connection of sorts. He had been a welder in the navy and this trade was a major part of an industrial pipe-fitter's day. Dad was the man I called at one o'clock in the morning when I had "flash burn" my first week welding joists. Flash burn is the unenviable condition of a burnt layer of cells on the retina caused by direct contact with the ultraviolet rays of an electric arc. I woke up with what felt like hot sand in my eyes, felt my way downstairs, and called him at his bar. When I told him about my suffering, he laughed and directed me to the tea bags in the kitchen cabinets.

"Tea bags?" I asked with a grimace.

"Yeah, just wet 'em, lay 'em on your eyelids and try to relax."

I followed his advice. I fell asleep and awoke the next day without a trace of the burn.

Connecting became my primary duty during my second year as an ironworker. Pete and I became good friends and he entrusted me with some smaller jobs overseeing a crew of four or five workers. I was given a Chevy S10 pickup truck to travel to job sites that needed finishing touches to close out our contractual obligations.

I had learned a trade. The $6.50 an hour had progressed to $10.50— not too shabby, but as a scab ironworker the wages we received were half of what the union boys earned. Every now and then we were lucky enough to land a rated job, a project that paid union rates to non-union outfits. While building a United States Post Office in Andover, Massachusetts, I was paid $22 an hour! My friends and I were livin' large. I had plenty of money to blow on booze and other things.

But the money, clearly, wasn't enough.

In August, 1987, the temperature stayed at close to 100 degrees. The notorious New England humidity hovered at 90 percent. I spent a lot of time lying on my back in a puddle of water, covered with leather to prevent catching on fire, welding over my head and thinking about my future.

The following month I was back at ULowell.

My friends, particularly Al, couldn't understand my decision to return to school. "You're making $22 an hour and you're going to school to be a scientist?" Al asked. I defended my decision, but he still thought I was crazy.

Working for Pete had been an invaluable experience. The times I spent burning my ankles with errant welding slag, driving to the hospital to stitch up an open gash—or to get a friend stitched up—or hanging from the bottom of a joist 40 feet above ground after losing my footing cannot be replaced. To discover what you want in any aspect of life, it is immeasurably helpful to know what you don't want. There are many jobs a young person can experience that will instill an appreciation for the advantages of having an education. Steel erecting is one of them.

(Even Peter eventually went back to school. He's now Dr. Peter Jaillet, D.C., a chiropractor.)

My desire to return to school was fueled not only by the hope for a better career, but also because I wanted a better lifestyle. During the two years I'd spent working construction, I'd abused drugs more than ever. Nothing too crazy; I wasn't selling my belongings to get a fix or missing work because I didn't know what day it was. But I blew a lot of money on pot, cocaine and alcohol. I never felt proud of this behavior, nor did I particularly enjoy staying up all night snorting coke and downing innumerable beers—or tequila and water, without ice—then making phone calls at 10 a.m. looking for just a little more before calling it a "night." But I did it just the same.

This type of all-nighter was typical for a number of my friends. It was an effort to fit in and push the "fun" envelope. Maybe I abused drugs to kill some sort of emotional pain. When I thought about it though, I didn't feel overly miserable or lonely.

The low point had come at a friend's party. We'd been drinking heavily all night, smoking lots of pot, and stuffing our noses with cocaine. Near the end of the night, severely intoxicated, I was still looking for a more intense high. Sitting in front of a mirror, I bent down to do yet another line. But I somehow lost control and hit the mirror so hard that the straw jammed up my nose and blood started dripping from it.

My friends had to prop me back up and help me gather what was left of my composure. Minutes later I wanted more, and I kept trying to open my wrapped razor blade, thinking it was a packet of cocaine. How I struggled to get one more line out of that razor blade.

Soon after I decided this life was not for me.

Continuing Education

The second time around, going to school was much more enjoyable—certainly more enjoyable than going to work.

I signed up for the school's Track II program. This route required fewer classes per semester, offered two or three additional basic classes freshman year, and allowed an extra year for completion—a structured five-year program.

My re-enrollment was accompanied by a change of focus, but I still kept an open major: Undeclared Science. I re studied trigonometry, chemistry and physics at a higher level. I was much more comfortable this time with an understanding of the hard, structured format of the sciences.

Perhaps Howie had done me a favor by guiding me into Liberal Arts the first time around. Had I gone straight into the sciences, I might have stayed in school and not experienced life as an ironworker.

I had another learning experience during this time: my first love. I met Sue Reponen and her daughter Katie in Gardner near the completion of my freshman year. Sue was 25, Katie was four, and I was a few days away from my 21st birthday.

In the two years that Sue and I were together, I discovered that romantic love is not enough to make a relationship last. There needs to be a mutual desire to move in the same direction emotionally. I had ambitions to go places but was not exactly sure where. I didn't know if my goal was a physical place or something less tangible. Sue would have been willing to go along, but that is not the same as wanting to. Moreover, Katie needed a father figure, not a fraternity brother.

The truth is that I remained the most important person in my life.

When Sue and I parted, I experienced for the first time the heartache that comes from hurting someone you love.

Around the same time I met Sue, I experienced another kind of heartache, the grief of losing someone you love. There would be no more pick-up street hockey in the furniture warehouse parking lot. No more late nights trying to guess which of the Boston Bruins players' numbers from the '79 roster we were drawing on each others' backs. No more laughs with my best friend. I was the last person to leave the wake when Rob was killed in a car accident on April 2, 1988.

When it happened, I was a student again but still working part-time for Pete. On the way to work one early Saturday morning, one of the crew members mentioned seeing the aftermath of an accident involving a blue, late model Camaro Z-28. Next to it was a sheet-covered body. The fact that it could be Rob's car never crossed my mind. That afternoon, as I headed off to Rob's house to hang out, a friend caught up with me in front of my home to ask if I had heard what happened to Rob. He didn't need to tell me.

With wide eyes and a loss of breath, I muttered, "He's dead?" A nod in reply and I suddenly felt an enormous pain right about where my heart is. I stormed back into my house, ripping a rusty iron railing out of its mooring in the process. I slammed the door to my room and cried hysterically, pounding on the wall so hard I could hear the plaster falling off its interior.

My best friend of the last 10 years had died. No experience could have prepared me for such a tragedy.

Rob's fiancé, Diana, was pregnant and due to have their first child in two months. When I saw her outside the funeral home being consoled by her family, she said to me, "You were his best friend, Paul. He talked about you all the time."

That night, after the funeral, I went home and wrote a poem:

> *Rob was once a friend of mine*
> *The kind I did appreciate*
> *With no more memories to be made*
> *Who is to blame? Such is fate*
> *He left behind a loving woman*

She was to be his wife
Rob would have been a loving father
Too bad he lost his life

Several days after the crash I remembered that on the ride home from work the day Rob died, I had noticed the beauty of the sunset, the peacefulness of a particular moment. Perhaps it was Rob telling me all was well, that life goes on.

Sometimes what you consider to be a coincidence can be a grace, a little help from our friends, a sign.

Some months later I stood in Rob's place at Robert Jr.'s baptism, with the little guy in my arms.

In August of that same year, I nearly joined Rob. Or perhaps it was Rob who intervened so that I would not.

I was on my way home from work (steel erecting for the summer) on a Friday afternoon, when I fell asleep at the wheel. My full-size pickup ran straight into a huge signpost, the type that supports the green overhead signs that span the highway. The impact was so centered that the bumper folded perfectly and its ends met each other on the opposite side of the signpost. The vehicle stopped dead. The force of the crash crammed the engine underneath the seat. Miraculously, I was tossed to the floor of the passenger side as the steering wheel ripped through the rear window. Had I worn a seatbelt, I would not be writing these words.

I remained conscious, though twisted and crunched on the floor. My lower back was killing me; I simply had to change positions. I had passed a friend of mine only moments before. Now he was on the scene, urging me to lie still, to stop struggling if I wanted to avoid further damage. I insisted on straightening myself out. I had to. My back was killing me.

I managed, with his help, to get myself through the now-open rear window and onto the bed of the truck. This new position—flat on my back—was far less painful than the wrenched contortion on the floor.

The paramedics arrived within minutes. They strapped me onto a stretcher, braced my back and neck, and whisked me off to Henry Heywood Memorial Hospital...again. The MRI diagnosed a compression fracture of the fourth lumbar vertebrae. The authorities told me how lucky I was to have avoided paralysis. Had the vertebrae slipped another millimeter, I'd be wheelchair bound.

The doctors recommended a fusion of the third, fourth and fifth lumbar vertebrae. I was not in a position to argue with them.

My father stood by my bed that evening with tears in his eyes. I was secretly warmed by his sadness.

Dad insisted on a second opinion. A few days later we traveled to the University of Massachusetts Medical Center in nearby Worcester. Two doctors there examined me, and both came to the same conclusion; no need for a fusion. A body cast and time off would sufficiently heal the broken vertebrae.

For the next two weeks I lay flat on my back at the medical center. No sitting up, no inclining, just flat on my back—a good time for introspection. One does not often spend 14 days, mostly solitary, without a change of scenery. I thought about school, about Sue and Katie, and even about my haphazard approach to life. The fact that this had been my fourth sleeping-at-the-wheel incident was more food for thought yet. *Am I a narcoleptic or something? I don't fall asleep in other weird places.* I pondered what problems I would have after recovery.

My hospital roommate was an older man who'd also broken his back in an auto accident. He told me that throughout his life he had continually varied his professions to keep his daily undertakings novel, to avoid a static existence. He had made a good living as a jeweler, a tire repair facility proprietor and an electronics shop owner, among other careers.

I had visitors most days. Trevor Beauregard, Glen "Toad" Ambrose and John Maillet came to see me one day. As soon as they walked in the door, Toad walked over and held up my bloody catheter bag in puzzlement. "What's this?" he asked.

"Put in down! Put it down! Put it down!" I demanded.

His expression conveyed ignorance, but he obliged and lowered the bag.

A catheter bag is a gravity-fed mechanism. Holding it over the host is not a good idea. When held above the bladder, the contents reverse themselves and feed back into the bladder. I was pissing into myself! When relief settled in, I explained the problem to the crew. Much laughter followed.

Not all catheter stories are funny ones. One night mine became clogged with a blood clot and I couldn't pee; I had some backed-up plumbing. The late-shift doctors removed the old catheter and installed a bigger one, right then and there. I was stone-sober, non-anesthetized, for the procedure, and it was remarkably painful. My latest roommate spoke up after the doctors left. "Man, that sounded like it hurt. That must've sucked."

Yeah, it sucked.

To fix the vertebrae, the staff implemented a nondescript hard cast from my armpits to my pubic hairs to remain in place for the next six weeks. The red plaster cast made a fitting backdrop onto which my sister Elaine painted a 360-degree skeleton, complete with a broken lumbar vertebrae #4.

Released from the hospital, and without much to do except scratch my incessantly itchy belly with a clothes hanger, I opted to tackle Stephen King's It. I had read 1,000 pages of the 1,100 page novel when my friend Andy got laid off from his construction job and began stopping by every morning to shoot the shit. We discovered before long that I could still get out and socialize, play pool and go for road trips.

I never did finish the book.

The accident occurred just before school convened for a new year. I missed the entire fall semester. I worked at my Dad's bar in the meantime. He gave me my first bartending lesson; I remember it well. He had me pour a customer's White Russian. Before long, the milk, Kahlua and vodka were all over the bar. Dad gave me a look that said, "What the hell are you doing?" and showed me proper mixing etiquette. Within a few weeks I had many of the customers' drinks on the bar before they even sat down.

In January, I returned to the University of Lowell campus.

I commuted to school for the first couple of weeks, until a bulletin board in Ball Hall posted an available room in a nearby house—$175 a month and just two minutes from campus. I immediately telephoned and visited the place that afternoon. Omicron Pi Fraternity.

A fraternity house. Hmmm? I never cared much for the Greek scene, but then again I knew next to nothing about it. "College boy" was the label most readily associated with the frat houses. I did not consider myself a "college boy" and I don't think anyone else did either. I did look the part, however: average height and weight, clean cut.

The guys I met that day—Dan, Mike, Scott and Paul—gave me a new perspective on fraternities. They were my kind of people. Relatively book smart, they liked to party and paid cheap rent. I moved right in. However, I still had some reservations about the Greek system. The whole initiation thing seemed so silly, along with the drunken games and the meaningless rituals around campus.

Hell week was unquestionably a test of mettle. It was not the beer-drinking, belly-busting, silly antic week most might assume. The fraternity was actually teaching lessons about loyalty, responsibility and family. We worked hard and learned the cannons of Fraternity. Brotherhood. Sure there was game-playing for the sake of the active brothers, but the activities were constructed to benefit what was literally "our house."

The Greek system at ULowell had been revoked from the university a few years before my arrival. Another fraternity had committed an act of severe hazing (this type of thing was the crux of my fraternal aversion) which forced the administration to discontinue a program started by O Pi and another House back in 1902. The fraternities and sororities were left to their own devices. They were no longer allowed to participate in school sponsored athletic events, charity drives or social functions and were no longer protected by the university when their social functions got out of hand.

The declaration had a positive side. O Pi was a local fraternity. We were not governed by a large conglomeration of other chapters whose bylaws spread over a multitude of regions and unknown brothers. The Omicron Pi Alumni Association, a corporation, owned the house we lived in, and our alumni board of directors, mostly from the area, made the major financial and administrative decisions. The active chapter did pretty much whatever it liked, whenever it liked. We were not the most community-conscious house; except for the Can Party we threw once each semester. To get in the door, a young partygoer was required to bring one non-perishable item to be donated to The House of Hope, a local homeless shelter.

I lived in that house for the next four years, engaging in typical fraternity brother stuff like intramural sports, studying and throwing and going to parties. There are many stories to tell, most of which don't belong in this book, but I'll include one by way of example: while I was getting high with a few friends in my room one night during a party, the subject of the door came up. It was one of those paper-thin-on-both-sides kinds of doors. I told Mike that someone could probably put their head through it if they tried. We exchanged grins as simultaneous fog lights turned on in our heads. I put mine down and ran into the door as hard as the three feet of running room provided would allow. The blast broke through the proximal side but only dented the outside. I backed up and charged again. This time my noggin poked through to the hallway. I pulled out, both ears bleeding, to see my friends roaring with laughter. I joined them in their merriment before we all headed downstairs to join the crowd.

The roofing, drywall and carpentry experience I had gained over the years, mostly working with my cousin T-Paul Johnson, came in handy at the fraternity house. ("T-Paul" is a French-Canadian thing. My maternal grandfather called me the same.) He taught me a great deal about handiwork. In exchange for my apprenticeship, I provided all the laughter.

For example, once, while siding a house, I stood on the highest ring of a six-foot stepladder. In need of nails, I turned and walked away, oblivious of my position in space. I hit the driveway hard and just as I started to laugh the ladder came down and the steel hinge struck me across the shin, removing all of the humor. T-Paul loved it!

And of course there was my first experience with a pneumatic nail gun. T-Paul gave me simple instructions on how to operate it and how he wanted a small overhanging wall to be assembled. He didn't make it 20 feet up the stairs before the wailing commenced. He ran down to find another one of his workers laughing hysterically, and to witness the index and middle fingers of my left hand fastened together with a 12-penny framing nail. I held them up at eye level and withdrew the steel, an excruciatingly painful affair.

Working under the influence of marijuana can be dangerous.

The active chapter of our fraternity was constantly improving the house with cheap labor—the brothers. I had taken the initiative and put myself in charge, unofficially, of house repairs. Most of the first floor rooms were dry-walled, including ceilings. I replaced many of the rafters and re-shingled the water-damaged roof to the garage. I installed a short string of stairs from the front porch to the side yard, and I must have replaced a dozen panes of glass throughout the house. I also fixed the door to my room. Because of my work, I was given the Ring Award my senior year, an annual award which goes to a brother for his demonstrated dedication to the house.

My Undeclared Science major became Mechanical Engineering during my sophomore year, the third year into the Track II program. I didn't have a particularly strong desire to pursue the field, but it seemed to be a fitting major for a mechanically inclined, number-smart kid like me. Moreover, I figured an engineering degree would be both honorable and utilitarian. Doors would open. My salary would be fat.

In *Zen and the Art of Motorcycle Maintenance*, Robert M. Pirsig wrote that the majority of college students do not attend institutions of higher learning for the sake of an education. They enroll and do the work for the sake of the grade and the diploma. The consideration that they might be learning how to be better writers and thinkers is only important if the end result is a better paying job. The intrinsic value of knowledge is not important to them. I was no exception to his observation.

The underlying theme remained that I, like most young people, was only interested in a better means of survival and not a better experience of being human.

I remained in the quest for a high paying career—for the sake of the money and nothing more. In sync with this line of thinking, I felt it would be wise to pursue a summer internship between my sophomore and junior years. I met with the ULowell job placement officer who, upon learning of my experience as an ironworker, thought I would be a perfect match with a particular company, Lincoln Electric, which recruited through our school. This company manufactured welding equipment—including, ironically, the machine that almost met its fate hanging off the back of the truck on Route 9.

I interviewed with the Boston office later that April. We discussed my history at Jaillet Welding, which included the tailgate story, as well as my current field of study and future ambitions.

The interviewers brought out some of their latest products that needed to be marketed in the area: the new SAE 250, a small, self-contained, medium duty MIG welder, and the Magnum MIG gun, the hand-held unit used in this type of welding process. They told me I would be "Magnum Man."

Suddenly it dawned on me; I was being interviewed for a *sales* position. All this time I thought I was there for an engineering slot they needed filled at their corporate headquarters in Cleveland, Ohio. The men told me that I was cut out for the job. Besides, I had a pickup truck. A perfect means for promoting product was having the machine with you on a sales call. I started two weeks later, at summer break.

The first day I spent my time studying the products and awakening my dormant welding skills. I also needed to learn the MIG process, which to that point I had seen but not practiced.

There are three major classes of hand-held welding practices: stick,

MIG and TIG. Stick welding is the simplest and most recognizable version. In basic terms, a small diameter steel rod, covered in flux (an agent that promotes stability in an otherwise volatile environment) carries an electrical voltage, which, upon contact with the workpiece, creates an electric arc so hot that both the welding rod and the workpiece melt together. The MIG process involves a coil of welding wire that also carries a voltage and is mechanically fed into the area being welded. A hand-held unit typically controls the process, and through this "gun," an inert gas such as argon or carbon dioxide is pumped around the weld puddle to act as the stabilizer, as does flux in the stick process. TIG welding involves a tungsten electrode that also carries a voltage and creates an electric arc strong enough to melt metals. This type of welding is used for precision and aesthetics. The first day welding was kinda fun. The second day it was not.

The U-joint on my truck blew and I broke down on the one-hour commute to work. I spent the morning hitchhiking, repairing and hitch-hiking. By 10 a.m. I was back on the highway. At 10:15 a.m. I was pulled over for an expired registration sticker. The resulting impoundment of my truck by the Concord Police Department forced me to make my way to the office via my right thumb, and not until about 4:30 p.m. Mr. Clausen told me to come back when I had my act together.

Dad didn't want me to lose the job, so the next day he shelled out $800 for a nice little salesman's car, a high mileage Chevy Cavalier, and I was back on the job by Thursday. Mr. Clausen was glad to have me back, despite the lack of a pickup to haul around a machine.

My introduction to professionalism came in the form of a business card. Mine came with the title *Technical Sales* listed under my name. A title was the big step in the direction of success. It went a long way toward boosting my self-esteem, and things continued to go well for me in the summer of 1990. I drove all over Massachusetts, New Hampshire and Connecticut promoting Lincoln Electric. In August, just before I was to head back to school, Mr. Clausen said, "When you come to Lincoln full time…"

"You mean I've already got a job lined up when I get out of school?" I asked.

"You're a diamond in the rough," he replied.

After that, I was confident that I would be working a real job for real money as soon as I received my degree. Engineering itself, I discovered, was not my cup of tea. It wasn't the difficulty of the tasks involved (I would graduate a member of the Pi Tau Sigma Mechanical Engineering Fraternity); it was just that the analytical part was so unappealing. I knew that after that summer, whether with Lincoln or not, I would find a job selling something technical. I would be a salesman with an engineering degree, a.k.a., a Sales Engineer. I enjoyed welding, I enjoyed meeting new people—and I would enjoy the money. This potential position took away a tremendous amount of pressure.

Lincoln cut back the following year on unnecessary expenditures and summer help was one of them. So I found myself, unexpectedly, looking for work. The American economy was suffering as a whole, particularly in Massachusetts. Massachusetts had the highest unemployment rate in the nation, and the city of Gardner had the highest unemployment rate in the state, something like 17 percent! With no work to be found in construction, engineering or sales, I took up Dad's offer to stay with him and my sister Elaine for the summer.

Dad had recently moved to Hilton Head, South Carolina, where he opened a pool hall. His motivation for starting the business was Elaine. She was, coincidentally (if there is such a thing), living in the area and floating between jobs. Dad wanted to help her out. Elaine agreed to manage the business, above which she could live in a makeshift apartment. The establishment's name came from both Dad's astrological sign, Taurus, and his heritage, French Canadian. Hence, Bullfrog's.

At the time, I was in a serious relationship with a woman from school, Jenny. (Her name has been changed to protect her innocence. She was the only innocent friend I had!) We had been together for a year or so and things were going great. Moving away for the summer would be hard on both of us, particularly Jenny; I was headed to a beach town!

I went to Hilton Head to earn money. I worked at the pool hall at night and framed houses during the day. Framing houses with these particular boys, complete with their heavy drawl, leather skin and bigotry, challenged me. The boys were not deeply educated and were perhaps intimidated. Their approach to dealing with a Yankee college kid was to treat me like I was subservient; they talked down to me, gave me the crappy jobs and played the old hit-the-roof-with-a-hammer-while-Paul's-head-is-right-under-it trick.

Allie, the second in command, liked to talk big about his adventures and his scrapping ability. One day he called me out to test mine. He grabbed my right arm in an attempt to apply the "say uncle" twist, but before he could make his demand, he was over my head being dropped onto the concrete floor. I did not mean to inflict injury, just to let it be known that I was no slouch. Allie missed the next day of work with a bruised hip. I heard it from the boss, who called me out that afternoon to see if I thought I was a "real tough guy." I said I wasn't. He was much larger than Allie, and I thought he might intend to teach me a lesson. My own intention was to stay healthy.

I proved myself not only through hard work and knowledge but also through my silence. One day, as three of us moved a wall by shouldering the spreaders (short two-by-four blocks placed between studs to hold them true), one of the spreaders broke loose, exposing the nail intended to hold it there. The heavy wall came down on me and the nail tore through my skin. I moved to the next spreader and kept going. A half-hour later Allie asked what the hell had happened to my shoulder. I told him and he said, "Man, we didn't even hear a peep out of you! Why didn't you say something?"

"What would be the point?" I asked.

The young kid who had put that wall together was fired on the spot. I tried to convince the boss not to can him, but he claimed that was one too many mistakes. Maybe that's why I hadn't said anything.

I made a friend that summer; his name was Keenan, a South African in town for the season. He and I went sailing one day in Dad's boat, a little two-man, 14 footer. As we launched off shore, a concerned woman who lived on the beachfront stood on her sandy porch and yelled to warn us of an upcoming storm. *Good news,* I thought. *Strong winds make for fun sailing.* Silly me.

We were nearly two miles out when we saw clouds developing over the island. We decided it would be best to start heading in; these clouds were darker than we had anticipated. As I came about to make our way toward land, a strong wind came upon us like a freight train and the boat capsized almost immediately. We had been in the process of putting some things into the cubbyhole when the winds hit, and the removable door was not yet in place. It floated away too quickly for us to retrieve it. Already in panic mode, we re-erected the craft in no time.

The wind was already blowing at what felt like more than 60 m.p.h. The mainsail and jib were flapping violently. I told my shipmate to take down the mainsail, warning him not to pull in excess so the line would not completely de-thread off the mast's end. Apparently he didn't process this information, because a moment later the entire sail assembly lay in the bottom of the boat. The jib lines had become grossly tangled, rendering it un-packable. The small bow sail continued to flap incessantly, until the fabric ripped halfway up alongside the guide wire that held it in place.

Then the lightning started. There were strikes in all directions. We discovered firsthand the effect lightning has as it hits the brine: it becomes a large splash of red and orange as the electric light is infracted through the kaleidoscopic spray of sea water. Crazy stuff that you don't, I mean, you *really don't,* want to see up close.

We could no longer see land; nor could we determine in which direction it lay. The storm seemed to come directly off the island, so we thought we were being blown further and further out to sea.

The sky was black and the rain pelted us horizontally. Keenan was clinging onto the mast, praying to God to spare his life. "Please let me live," he pleaded aloud. I was with him, sharing the fear that we might not survive. I clung to the starboard side, ballasting as best I could as the forceful winds repeatedly threatened to capsize our boat by merely blowing against the hull. The thought of capsizing again terrified me as the cubbyhole remained exposed and would fill the hull with water.

While Keenan prayed for his life, I saw a bolt of lightning strike not far from us. It struck and crackled with incredible volume. My friend's eyes lit up with the electric shock. The mast, to which he was still clinging, carried the ambient voltage and acted as a lightning rod, something neither of us had considered in the commotion.

"I've been hit!" he exclaimed.

"No, man, but it hit right over there!" I said, in an attempt to reassure him that he was still alive.

We clung for our lives for nearly an hour. The sky to the south of us—or at least what I assumed to be south—finally began to clear and the wind and rain subsided. "Thank God this thing's about to end," I said.

But the calm did not last five minutes before the torrents returned. The starboard side mast line broke loose at its anchor. For another 45 minutes, our little boat and spirits were tormented. More lightning, more rain, more wind and more prayers. We held on and literally rode out the storm.

When the storm did finally clear, there wasn't much left to work with to make our way homeward. The mainsail was intact, but to restring the lead would require an intentional capsizing, which I still feared might sink the vessel. The jib was ripped, but not completely. Keenan held it as open as possible as I took hold of both the rudder and the broken mast line to hold the mast erect. This allowed us to use the jib.

Eventually a slight glimpse of land became visible in the distance. We sailed toward it for about an hour, forearms and hands suffering in the process.

Then a boat approached, coming directly at us from behind, from further out to sea. It was a chartered fishing boat that had also weathered the storm. The clients and captain were shocked to see such a tattered little rig making its way toward land. They threw us a line and towed us the remaining three or four miles back to shore.

It was after the boating incident that I began to wonder if my life was being repeatedly spared for some greater purpose.

The Big Change

As soon as I left the construction site for the classroom, the nine-to-five world seemed far away. I reminded myself that I'd be working again before long. I really thought I was ready to start a career, so it helped to know that an engineering degree and the prospect of a high paying job were not far off. I began to relax about my studies. I displayed a certain degree of apathy toward my classes—engineering more than others—confident that I would soon enter the workforce as a salesperson. This attitude manifested itself in my less-than-stellar grades. I needed only to graduate to secure my job with the Lincoln Electric Company and to get the paychecks moving in my direction. In the meantime, Jenny and I were spending a lot of time together and we truly enjoyed nearly every moment. I thought she was the one.

During the first week of the spring semester, Lincoln Electric flew me, first class, to their Cleveland headquarters to interview for a full-time sales position. I had met with the company recruiter several weeks earlier at ULowell's placement office.

The Cleveland interviewing process was a confidence-boosting, all-day affair. Six executives, men and women, met with me one by one to ask questions about work ethic, background and social awareness. They also asked about my family life, and I responded as honestly as necessary; I avoided some of the facts.

Harry Handlin, company president at the time, was the final interviewer of the day. He sat me down in his grand, mahogany-stained office and asked me to explain my approach toward responsibility.

"Well, sir, I don't believe in the phrase, 'No can do,'" I said with sincere confidence.

His smile slowly filled the room. "You said the right thing, Paul. Turn around."

Behind me hung a large circular poster stating the company's sales campaign slogan for the year: CAN DO IN '92!

I was unable to hide my pride. Not once that day had I seen or heard the phrase. It just seemed like the right thing to say, and I spoke it in earnest. Then and there, I knew that if I wanted it, his seat would be mine someday.

"I'm prepared to offer you a job today, Paul," he said.

"Thank you, sir," I responded.

He sent me back to the human resource officer who had recruited me, Rita Sherwood. I felt so proud strutting back toward her office. *I have the right stuff.* With just a few simple spoken words, I had The Big Cheese rooting for me.

When I returned to human resources, the other potential recruit who had been answering questions that day was there, bearing a big grin. Katie Jereza, an attractive woman of Filipino/Irish descent, had also been offered a job. We were happy for each other and looked forward to working together.

I told Ms. Sherwood that Mr. Handlin had offered me a job before the interview in his office had ended, thinking that he didn't even need the others' opinions. She told me that he already had their recommendations before offering me a position. *Damn.* A small buzz kill, but, hey, I still had the right stuff. She then asked me if I was prepared to accept their offer of a $27,000 salary plus a yearly bonus, which she could not guarantee but would likely be around $9,000. A total of $36k a year!

Holy shit! Someone's gonna give me $36,000 a year!

To show some bravado I told her she would have my answer by Monday.

"Looks like no one wants a job today," she muttered. Katie had offered the same response, but we knew damn well that we'd be accepting the offers.

I returned to school as the envy of the mechanical engineering department. For most of that final semester, I was the only one with a job. By the time May rolled around, only a handful of the other students had secured corporate positions. Most of the jobs, like mine, were in sales.

My senior project design team consisted of four less-than-technically-dominant minds, including my own. Our task was the same as that of the other three teams: to redesign the automated motion mechanisms of a Ford car seat. We had to design four separate and independent ranges of motion: forward/backward, up/down, recline/incline and lumbar support. The project spanned the entire year and took us through all the necessary steps from product design to manufacture.

Demonstration day demonstrated that our team wasn't the cream of the engineering crop. Our seat only moved in the forward/backward range, via a computer keypad entry of the team's design, which I had built. The kicker: of the 16 students in the manufacturing design class, we were the only ones with jobs waiting for us upon graduation.

Ms. Sherwood's assistant forwarded me the appropriate paperwork when I accepted the position as sales trainee for the Lincoln Electric Company. Weeks later she gave me contact information for Brent Ireland, a young man with an electrical engineering degree from Penn State who had also accepted a job as a sales trainee. I could speak to him about a rooming situation for the nine-month training program.

Brent and I moved into an apartment in Willowick, Ohio, just a few miles outside of the Lincoln manufacturing plant and office headquarters in Euclid, east suburban Cleveland. The company had helped us to find the apartment building, which was popular with the yearly rotating sales trainees. Two other Lincoln rookies, Lisa and Mary Lou, were in our building.

There were 12 of us: Brent, me, Lisa, Mary Lou, Katie, Kelcie, Matt, Brendan, Eric, Mark and two Lincoln Canada trainees, Will and Joel. We were an energetic and dynamic group of young people. We were all fresh out of school, eager to build careers and enjoy new found "wealth."

We played ultimate Frisbee, tackle football and drinking games and worked side by side for six months. We discovered which taverns had free food or cheap buffalo wings on different nights. I joined a hockey team, playing center and left wing. (My goaltending days had ended shortly after my dismissal from ULowell's team.) I even scored a hat trick, three goals in a single game, early in the season. Life was grand.

Training for the first three months consisted primarily of learning the products and acquiring the skills necessary to accomplish most types of welding: stick, MIG and TIG. This was a challenge for everyone, men and women alike. I was the only experienced welder in the group.

We were given projects or processes to master over the course of a given week. I usually passed the rudimentary tests in a day or two and was encouraged to help the others. So I did, particularly the ladies. Not because they couldn't weld, but because they were, well, attractive women. And they were dressed in leather. Granted, it was dirty, scummy, greasy, welding leather. Lisa was most definitely my favorite and I could often be found in her little booth, not so much to help her welding skills as to enjoy her company.

Lisa was 22. A suburban Pittsburgh native, she had spent most of her life in Beaver Falls, Pennsylvania, home of Joe Namath. She then spent four years away at school. Like Brent, she was a Penn Stater. She had earned a chemical engineering degree but didn't have much interest in a career in that field; the same could be said for each of us.

Lisa had dark brown hair, full of curls, a semi-permanent smile and a small, firm physique. She loved to laugh, which is what I liked most about her. She was often the center of attention at whatever social event we attended. We hit it off from the start. We were nearly inseparable.

I think what really sold me on her was how well she played the radio game, when you hit the car radio scan button and have to name the artist while a song is playing just before the radio moves on to the next one. She was ever-so-slightly better than me, winning maybe 51 percent of the time. I think it was only because there were too many country stations in and around Cleveland. I'd always nail the classic rock tunes, she'd get the country songs and we'd split 80s pop.

At the conclusion of our 12-week welding program, the group was given standard welding certification tests. Most of us passed them on the first try. Some had to take them twice. Thanks to my experience, I received a perfect score. The Lincoln Welding School presented me with an "Honor Roll" belt buckle, which I lost soon after.

About this time, *60 Minutes* aired a piece on Lincoln Electric. The Leslie Stahl feature was one of few that glorified its topic. Brent and I had a party at our place that night to commemorate our great company and our great potential to become its future leaders. It was known throughout Lincoln Electric that the sales department was taking control of what had previously been in the hands of the founders and engineers.

It was the company's unique system of rewarding workers that had deemed it worthy of national attention. Piecework, or Incentive Management, as James Lincoln termed it (he also wrote a book about it by that title), paid consistently high bonuses at year's end to all Lincoln employees, save the executives. The more product a worker put out at his or her work station, the higher their bonus at the end of the year. It was a very efficient system in its time. When the *60 Minutes* program aired in 1992, Lincoln boasted the highest paid factory workers in the world. Even in the late '60s, the bonus at Lincoln could be as high as 122 percent. That's 122 percent of a year's wages. It is said that car dealers would line up new Corvettes and other sporty cars outside the factory on Bonus Day, the first Friday of December.

During my tenure, however, bonuses were in the 50-60 percent range, and the factory workers still earned a comfortable living. Salespeople were paid a fluctuating salary dictated by the Cleveland Industrial Index, regardless of which city you lived in and serviced. A metro New York City employee would be faced with the city's exorbitant costs of living while a salesperson in Tulsa had it made. On average, the sales department earned typical industry market value with the added profit-sharing bonus.

Part of our training program was a two-week stint working among the factory personnel. The trainees were required to perform the tasks that the factory workers performed, including welding, painting, assembling, etc. The program was designed to build an appreciation for those whose sweat, muscle and skill went into each product that we would be representing in our white shirts and bold ties. It also was intended to promote a sense of family within the company.

The first week, I welded base frames for one of our large engine-driven, portable machines, the SAE 250. This machine was the workhorse of the steel erection and field pipe welding industry. Peter Jaillet had employed these in his fleet of machines. It was an SAE 250 that hung off the back of his Ford Crew Cab that memorable day.

The second week, I worked an assembly line and handled a sub-assembly of the Ranger 8, a midsize, gasoline-engine-powered welder/generator. These were the first two weeks of tiring manual labor I had done in more than a year.

On the opposite side of a slight roll on eastbound Interstate 90—the "Shoreway" it's called in Cleveland—near the East 185th Street exit, a fire truck and ambulance were parked on the median attending an accident. As I came over the ridge, my head bobbed and woke me up. I saw the lights of the parked fire truck about 50 feet in front of me and cut the wheel sharply to the right, ducking toward the passenger's side. I had apparently learned the crash position from previous accidents. It came naturally now, without thought.

Once again, I was not wearing a seatbelt—but this time it would have helped. The impact with the fire truck tossed me from the car onto the highway. In mid-ejection, my leg was snagged in the door jam.

I have only one memory of the incident before waking after the 12-hour life-saving surgery. Lying in the ambulance, the one that had already been on the scene, I remember the EMT cutting up the length of my jeans. I may have been in a state of shock—I was not feeling much pain—but I knew damn well this was a bad sign.

Transitions

Dr. Laurence Bilfield, the orthopedic surgeon who helped save my life, was standing at my side when I regained consciousness. He immediately informed me that I had been in a car accident, had received multiple injuries and was in stable condition. I'd woken up in hospitals before, so I wasn't too panicky. As my world came into focus and I processed the given information, what concerned me most was the respiratory tube inserted down my throat. I had so many questions, but the tube prevented me from asking them. And as I was secured to the table with IVs in each arm, I couldn't write either. Dr. Bilfield understood my frustration and asked that I wait to regain strength and cognition before looking for answers. The tube, he said, would be removed in 24 hours.

I examined my predicament: left leg fully dressed in bandages along with three stainless steel rods sticking out of either side of my tibia and fibula; an incredible headache (resulting from a first degree concussion); a total body ache that rendered me unable to move. These things happen when you are ejected from a car at 60 m.p.h. The doctor assured me that I would be fine, that there was no major internal damage; I would recover.

For the next nine days I administered my own morphine by pushing a button on a device that released a set amount of the painkiller into my system intravenously, up to three times per hour. Morphine took away some of the pain, but it also brought on some nasty nightmares. In one, I was snorting salt for what seemed like an eternity. The deep-sleep sensations felt incredibly real and painful.

What I did not expect, while lying awake from six in the morning until three the next morning, was the degree of pain I endured. The only redeeming aspect of the pain in my left leg was that it held my attention while the rest of my body throbbed.

Cleveland was a 10-hour ride from Gardner, and most of my friends and family back home weren't able to visit. My friends from Lincoln, however, spent their lunch breaks and evenings with me. The first week they were all in town. Then Lincoln gave the trainees two weeks off for the holidays. As expected, my friends traveled to their respective homes in far off cities. A few of the local people from the sales department kindly spent time in my room.

Rita Sherwood, the human resources officer, was the center of continual gossip throughout the sales force, and my mouth was as guilty as the next. Nevertheless, when the chips fell and I needed her help, she gave me her full support. Early in my hospital stay, a gang-shooting victim was admitted into my room, and his friends were too loud and inconsiderate for me to get any rest. I asked Rita to get me into another room as soon as possible. The nurses moved me within the hour.

She went further by allowing Lisa to spend entire afternoons with me after she and the others visited at lunchtime. By this point, Lisa and I had developed a wonderful relationship and become romantically involved despite each of us having a significant other at home. It was a fantastic and unstoppable relationship. We were too compatible not to develop such a bond. Rita, along with the entire sales force and fellow trainees, was ignorant of our true relationship. But she knew we had a special friendship.

Without much family around, Lisa gave me the love I needed at the time. She made the pain easier to accept.

My father made the trip from South Carolina. His initial reaction was typical Dad. "Looks like you won't be playing center any more," he delivered with a chuckle. I laughed with him.

This was the fifth time he was visiting me in a hospital, and interestingly enough, each incident was more serious than the one before it: I fell off the back of a moving car and got a concussion at age 12, an overnight stay; at 15 years of age, I said the wrong thing to the wrong person, which resulted in another overnighter; there was the bicycle incident at 18, a three-day stint; the broken back at 22, with its two-week lay-up; and this one, at age 25, which did not surprise Dad.

Dad rubbed lotion on my mysteriously hardened and dry right foot. He scratched my incessantly itchy back. He applied cold compresses to my forehead. His presence there meant a lot to me. He could only stay for two days, but he promised to come back before too long.

I lost a great deal of blood and experienced vampire-like sensations in that hospital room. The nurse confirmed that I was a full four pints short. I was not surprised. The blood shortage combined with the morphine left me extremely weak in both body and mind. When the staff finally provided me with two pints of blood, I felt incredibly energized, like a rechargeable battery back in its holster. Within an hour I was more alert and powerful. I wanted more and more blood, but there wasn't enough. The next day I was given a third and fourth pint. Next to the daily visits from friends, the blood offerings were the highlight of my care.

At one point, my sodium level became dangerously low, so low that further dilution would compromise the common functions of my central nervous system. The staff carefully monitored it. The prescribed fix was a reduction in fluid intake to prevent further dilution. This meant no more water for me. Liquids were not allowed at a time when all of me longed for them. For two days, I was not allowed to drink *anything*. I was given a wet Q-Tip several times daily to moisten my mouth. Once a day I was given a few grapes for nourishment and salvation. Those grapes lasted *soooo* long.

The six screws that held my heavily-damaged leg together stuck out two inches on either side of my lower leg. Both my fibula and tibia had compound fractures in several places. My femur had also broken cleanly at its mid-section, which meant a steel rod had to be permanently installed down the center of the bone where marrow had once been. In the crash, my shin had folded forward, and both bones were shattered. The sharp edges had ripped through the arteries and veins in my calf muscle, creating some serious circulation problems.

The leg bandages were changed twice daily—an extremely painful experience. I took the liberty of directing the nurses through the process. "Lift with one hand below the knee and one below the heel, not too fast."

Only once did I actually see the carnage during the dressing. The sight was gruesome, although in my drugged state I hardly wavered. All of my skin had been peeled away from the lower leg to lessen the pressure on the arteries caused by the swelling. Almost my entire lower leg was now exposed muscle: red, swollen, vulgar. My left foot was white and looked dead. The damaged arteries failed to circulate the necessary amount of blood.

The medical staff began using a Doppler metering device to detect circulation when manual efforts failed. The unit's hand-held wand emitted radio waves, which were reflected by a pulse—if there was one—back to the wand. The circulatory status was determined by an audible tone. On the fifth day, there was no pulse, causing the meter to emit a dull buzz. I underwent surgery the next day in an effort to restore the desperately needed circulation.

I awoke from the four-hour surgery with a new set of sutures, this time on my inner right thigh. The surgeons had removed a major artery to answer a more urgent need for blood in my left calf muscle. The docs broke out the Doppler meter again and I heard a distinct pulse—*music* to my ears. Later that day the signal was still there. My leg, and my spirits, remained intact.

But an hour later, the soothing signal perished, and the doctors were prompted to perform more surgery. This time a prosthetic vein was implanted. Just before the end of visiting hours, I failed the audible test on the first try—the hollow buzz had returned. The next morning I went into surgery for a third time.

Dr. Laurence Bilfield and Dr. Terry King, the surgeons who performed the original life-saving operation, also performed the latest. They returned the pulse once again, only to have it fail within the hour. Three operations, under full anesthesia, began to take their toll. I became very weak, as well as discouraged and disoriented. Still, I was scheduled to go under the knife again later that afternoon.

The fourth four-hour surgery mirrored the previous three. Circulation was restored, but only temporarily. Once again, the meter gave hope, then took it away. Dr. Bilfield, with his excellent bedside manner, approached me late that evening and informed me that things weren't looking so good; amputation was necessary. He asked if I would sign a contract allowing the surgeons to remove my left leg below the knee.

Chop off my leg? What a decision! But the days of pain and disappointment made it easier than I would have thought. I signed the paper with minimal resistance; I wanted to move ahead with the matter. In a sober state I believe I would have cried my eyes dry, but having been through several operations in such a short time, I had neither sufficient emotion nor energy to shed more than a few tears. I just accepted it. The good doctor informed me of all the things I could still do as an amputee. Some of his former patients enjoyed softball, some played golf. One had even run a marathon. His words helped reduce the grief to some degree.

What really kept my spirits up was the basic realization that I wasn't dead. Others were surely worse off than I was.

Word spread fast to my friends and throughout the sales department. Lincoln's CEO, Don Hastings, came to visit the next day, a Sunday. He brought a bouquet of poinsettias so big they didn't even fit in my room. Instead, they were respectfully displayed in the lobby and I never did see them. Mr. Hastings told me about Mr. Mackenbach, the new company president, who had suffered the same impairment.

"You don't understand, Mr. Hastings. They're going to cut my leg off," I said.

"Yes, Paul, I understand. Mr. Mackenbach, believe it or not, has a prosthetic leg."

"Really?!" I almost *didn't* believe it! I had seen this 62-year-old man walk busily around the company halls, going up and down stairs in his briskly efficient manner. Learning that he wore a prosthesis gave me more than a glimpse of promise. *If Mr. Mackenbach can get around so well, and be so successful, then maybe I can too.*

On my final trip to the operating room, for my own therapeutic benefit, I joked with the staff when they admitted me into surgery. "Goodbye, foot," I said as they administered the anesthetic. I wanted to feel good again, both mentally and physically.

When my eyes opened in the recovery room, they immediately steered toward what was left of my left leg. My new stump—five inches below my knee, professionally referred to as a "residual limb"—was heavily bandaged and I was unable to bend it. Strangely, my gaze was not one of horror, which might be expected. Instead, it was one of inquiry. *So this is what it's like to be amputated?*

While staring at my newly found form, I had another realization: I felt no *pain*. The pain I had endured and suffered through for the last nine days was gone. No pain! I instantly felt better about the whole one-legged thing.

Gratefully, Dad and Paty were standing to my right when I came around. If she could have, I know my mother would have been there, too. She came out a couple of weeks later with three of my father's four sisters. Their visit reminded me that family is precious.

Friends and family at home sent many letters of support. People I had not heard from in years wrote or phoned my room. I shed tears every day as more and more letters came pouring in. Priceless encouragement.

My cousin, T-Paul Johnson, and a mutual friend, Gino Agnelli, made the drive from Gardner to Cleveland for a supportive visit. In classic T-Paul style, he walked in the room—a total surprise to me—and rattled off about a dozen no-arm-no-leg jokes. *What do you call a guy with no arms and no legs in a pile of leaves? Russell. What do you call a guy with no arms and no legs in a pool? Bob.* T-Paul had me laughing for the first time in days.

T-Paul was still there a couple of days later when I walked for the first time on my IPOP (immediate post-operative prosthesis). I could barely hobble 20 feet without running out of steam. And all the while I struggled not to shit myself as T-Paul attacked mercilessly.

"What's the matter? First day on your new leg?"

We all laughed. The nurse hit him.

T-Paul owned a diner in Gardner, and he constantly bombarded his customers with jokes. And, believe me, they pretty much all sucked. Of course, he laughed every time he told one of them.

After endless examination of my residual limb, which I have aptly dubbed "Stumpie," I decided that it looked a lot like Dino from *The Flintstones*. This discovery gave rise to simple entertainment as I wiggled what was left of my leg and made little Dino "yipes" to pass the time. This attitude allowed me to see the lighter side of my circumstance. It wasn't always easy, and I would never say it came naturally. It was a choice. Some nights I chose not to have that attitude; some nights I chose to cry.

One night as I lay in bed I made another choice. I decided to make the most of my predicament. I decided that I would find a way to show everyone who would want to see that a disability is only as limiting as you allow it to be.

I spent five weeks in both Mount Sinai Hospital, where the surgeries took place, and Euclid Meridia, a rehab hospital. Then it was time to go home and to start facing the challenge of believing that I, an individual, am not too small to make some sort of positive difference in our world.

My actions can make a difference, I promised myself. By being myself and setting an example of what it means to see the bright side of every predicament, I can shine a light on the people I meet.

Standing On One Leg

Released by my caregivers, I returned to my apartment and headed straight for the shower. *Time to clean up and get going.* In front of the mirror that morning, clean-shaven and energetic, I had a shocking moment of enlightenment. While combing my hair, jigging to Aerosmith's *"Dream On,"* I found myself joyfully singing completely out of tune, preparing for my day's agenda—as happy as I had been every other morning before the crash. I hadn't forced the positive attitude; it had just come over me.

Then it hit me like a two-door Mazda slamming into a parked fire truck—*I was standing there on only one leg!*

I was the same person I had been five weeks ago. I had lost a physical part of my being, but my spirit remained whole. I felt such tremendous relief that it defies words. At that moment, I knew—*I knew*—that my future would be every bit as prosperous as I had ever imagined. There was no reason to consider myself anything less than the person I had always been. I even *felt* special…in every positive sense imaginable.

Back in the Ballgame

I returned to work on a Saturday, six weeks after the crash. It was great to be back with the team again—back on my feet again, or back on my foot again, as the case may be. Stumpie was not yet able to bear weight since I still had an open wound from the trauma. (The IPOP only lasted a few days.) I was on crutches, but I was myself, and nothing less.

I'd been back for less than a week when the group began packing up their belongings. The friends I had made were being sent to their chosen or designated sales territories. The sales department had a bottom line to meet and wanted as much presence in the field as they could muster. Lisa was no exception, but I was delighted to learn she had picked the Cleveland district sales office in which to perform her duties. Her decision had nothing to do with me. She actually liked the city but had based her decision on her family and her one-year-old niece—and her boyfriend. They were all back in Beaver Falls, just two hours to the east. But she was around, and that was all that mattered to me.

Rehabilitation was my number one responsibility for the next few months. Number two was to cover the training materials I had missed while out for six weeks. Rehab took 10 to 15 hours a week; I spent 25 to 30 hours at work. I soon fulfilled my training requirements, so to keep me busy while I wrapped up my rehab, the company put me to work in the automation department, learning about robotics.

Manufacturers interested in purchasing a Lincoln robotic system would send in a dozen sample parts to be test welded with one of our units. My job was to program a robot to produce a welded item in the most time-efficient manner possible, weld quality notwithstanding. The job was particularly fitting for me since I lacked a prosthetic leg for much of this time. I spent most of my programming time sitting. Even so, life on one leg was challenging. Getting around on crutches in the snow, for instance, was difficult. And there were times I got off the couch thinking I still had two feet: Face, meet Carpet.

Undoubtedly, there would be more challenges, but I had my mind, my spirit and, most importantly, my freedom to choose.

A friend of mine had learned the value of freedom the hard way, about the same time I learned that my body parts were on loan.

This friend shared many of my youthful memories, both inside and outside legal boundaries. He was the guy who had let me ride his mini-bike. He was also the guy who had introduced me to cocaine. A few months before my latest accident, he had gone to New York City with a couple of drug-dealing friends to pick up a considerable amount of the stuff—a kilo. They were pulled over for some type of traffic violation, the drugs were discovered, and each man was placed under arrest and charged with interstate drug trafficking.

In the Commonwealth of Massachusetts, the mandatory sentence for this offense is 10 years in the state penitentiary. Because each of the men refused to finger the others, they all faced prosecution. My friend, anticipating a joy ride and freebie high, was sentenced to maximum security prison to begin his 10-year penance.

When we spoke for the first time, two months after his sentencing and six weeks after the accident that claimed my left foot, we exchanged horror stories and wondered who had it worse. At the time I wasn't sure.

I traveled home to Massachusetts in March, three months after the accident, to visit friends and family and to show them that I'd be just fine. We all got together at the Napoleon Club in Gardner, in the heart of a small section of town known as Little Canada. (I had played Little League baseball for the Nap Club. We sucked—and were 0-15 in my third and final year.) At the party, one long-time friend offered the greatest honor I could ever hope for. Gary Lafrenier said, "Poop, if any of us had to lose a leg, I'm glad it was you." He had my attention. "You're the only one who could've handled it."

Before landing the job at Lincoln I had been strongly drawn toward the idea of beginning my career in the Pacific Northwest. I had sent most of my résumés to companies like Boeing, Intel and Microsoft. Rejection letters from nearly three dozen companies had covered the walls of my fraternity house bedroom.

When I completed my latest rehabilitation and obtained a permanent prosthetic, John Stropki, Lincoln's Vice President of Sales, asked me to make a decision about where I would like to be placed. My choices were New York City or Portland, Oregon. I suddenly had a chance to write my own ticket to the geographic area I was so interested in. I sat in front of the typewriter and began to formalize my request. All but the last sentence was complete. "All things considered I would like to go to…"

I stopped and pondered for sometime. It was actually a difficult decision. Among other things, I thought about Jenny, my truly wonderful girlfriend back in Lowell. Jenny was an extremely beautiful, blond, green-eyed woman with a bright future. She was as true to me as I could ever have hoped for, and I sincerely enjoyed being with her. Jenny, from anyone's perspective, was the catch of a lifetime. There was no opening in the Boston office, so New York City was as close as I could get to her.

Mr. Stropki had made it clear, without having explicitly said so, that New York City would also be in the best interest of my career. New York would provide a more challenging district in which to sell, boosting my company appeal, and a salesperson was needed there more than in Portland.

I typed NEW YORK on the paper.

"Good choice," I heard someone say from directly behind me. It was Mr. Stropki. How long he'd been there I'll never know.

Lisa and I had developed a deeper romantic friendship in the preceding months. True, we each had very significant others in our lives and visited them often. She saw hers more than I, because of proximity. Nevertheless, we spent several nights a week together. Our relationship had been strengthened by her ever-so-committed presence when I truly needed a friend; she was always there for me. The time had come, however, for us to part. I had to move on to a sales office and a career. I told her not long before departing that I had chosen New York City for reasons primarily to do with a life with Jenny. She never tried to persuade me otherwise. She had Joe waiting for her.

We made love the morning I left town. The act brought up a great deal more emotion than either of us expected. Later, as she headed out the door, I stood at the threshold and called her back. "Lisa, I've got something to tell you. I love you."

"Oh, Paul," she responded, misty-eyed.

Neither of us said more. We just cried in each other's arms. The moment was brief and much too painful. She got into her car and drove off. Minutes later the telephone rang.

"I just wanted you to know that I love you, too. I just couldn't say it," she confessed. Then she called again. This time she said cheerfully, "I can't believe it, Stevie Wonder's '*I Just Called To Say I Love You*' is playing on the radio!"

We laughed; it was such a perfect closing to that chapter of my life.

Something Bigger

Crying, laughing, thinking, celebrating; I did 'em all during the emotional nine-hour journey to New Jersey, home of Lincoln's Metro New York office. Thoughts of Lisa, Jenny and career jostled for position. I did my best to focus on the latter for therapeutic reasons.

I was headed to the greatest metropolis in the world to show my stuff. The office was short one salesperson and in need of immediate manpower.

There wasn't much time for learning the system before the boss threw me to the lions. I picked up on the necessary survival tactics: quick wit, quickly returned calls and quick moves among aggressive Jersey drivers (I already had that). The nerves that I had when I arrived quickly dispersed. Selling product in that competitive sector, like anywhere else, I'm sure, was a matter of befriending the natives. Selling was the easy part. The hard part was getting excited about it.

Not long after settling into my territory, I began to second-guess my career choice. I realized that if I continued to work for Lincoln, not much would change in my life over the next 40 years. When this theme came to mind, I told myself that a prosperous career and plenty of money—complete with pride and prestige—should take precedence over any mundane attitudes I might have toward my career. A family, presumably with Jenny, a big house and a nice car would do it. I would be happy because I had reached these goals. I could achieve this success by climbing someone else's ladder.

My boss, Charlie Wright, didn't help the situation. He was demeaning toward me and the others in the office—a trait I do not particularly appreciate. On my third day in the office, Charlie tested me with a technical question, which, of course, I answered incorrectly. His response was a sarcastic, "Which leg do I kick you in?"

Now, you can talk smack about the leg thing all you want—if you're a friend. But I couldn't believe this authority figure, whom I had hoped to respect, showed such blatant disrespect to me. I went into another room to sort out my feelings and come up with a prudent course of action. What I felt like saying was, *"Which eye do I hit you in?"* Clearly, that would not have been an exceptionally brilliant move, nor is it my style.

In the end, I let it ride. But I got my two cents in the following week.

Underlings of Charlie Wright were traditionally initiated into the office with a night of martinis at the local TGIFriday's. The other salesmen in the office joined Charlie and me for what turned out to be much more gin than I had expected. The boys left early and Charlie and I stayed to discuss "important things" for a while. Before long he asked what I thought of him. With alcohol-induced honesty, I replied, "I think you're an asshole."

My relationship with Charlie improved after that, but I still didn't like him. I am thankful that he helped me see more of what's important, by making it clear that there were other things I could be doing with my time. Unwittingly, Charlie fueled my resentment toward a corporate lifestyle.

I began to resent the idea of devoting my life to a career for the sake of a paycheck. I wanted a greater, deeper purpose. I felt restless and empty. With each sales call I made, I felt more and more that I was on the wrong path. Customers' welding problems were of no interest to me whatsoever. Sure, I would garner some satisfaction when I resolved the issue at hand. For example, I was the first salesperson in the Northeast to sell a robot. But I didn't sleep any better for it. Each morning I questioned my circumstances and myself. During my rookie year as a ladder-climber, it was extremely difficult to find any motivation to shine in the customer's office. *What purpose am I serving by selling this guy a red machine?* I couldn't find one.

Linda Nelson had bought me a pair of skis and boots for Christmas during my senior year of high school and had unleashed the skier in me. I skied about three dozen times, over an eight-year period, without ever taking a lesson. I was always the out-of-control guy that the competent skiers loathed.

In Stowe, Vermont, on December 11, 1993, the last day of the first full year since my accident, I discovered that my skiing ability, or lack thereof, was not terribly affected by my impairment. This was true even with the use of a low-grade prosthetic—my first leg was a crappy one. Skiing was so much easier than other activities I had tried for one simple reason: gravity. Gravity produced nearly all the momentum needed to enjoy the sport. Most importantly, my body weight consistently pressured the socket, which, with the assistance of duct tape, kept my residual limb from losing its fit. Suspension became a problem only when I crashed—and this happened all too often, not because of my gimpy leg, but because I sucked to begin with.

The suspension system employed to hold the leg in place plays a critical role in allowing someone like me to participate in running or skating at a reasonably competitive level. In these sports it is the pull from behind at the initiation of the stride, and the subsequent inertia-driven pull at the end of the stride, that causes the leg to loosen. Inertia, one might say, is the enemy of suspension.

While skiing, my prosthetic and residual limb were in close contact with limited relative motion. I still relied on lots of duct tape for added suspension.

The first run showed me that I had retained all the "skills" I once possessed as a non-disabled skier. That winter I skied a few more times, and besides some discomfort on the lift ride caused by the weight of the ski and boot tugging on my stump, everything was great. Late in the season I traveled to the Eastern Regional Disabled Skiing Championships in Waterville Valley, New Hampshire to see if I stood a chance as a competitive gate-chaser. The U.S. team was not there, but I didn't see anyone much better than I was.

As the last racer came by, I remembered lying in the hospital bed, thinking about what I'd be able to do with my life, and what opportunities might present themselves when I made my way back into the pack. I decided to pursue disabled ski racing.

Meanwhile, Jenny and I were re-establishing a strong relationship. I drove four hours to Massachusetts every other weekend to spend time with her. Moving in with me wasn't an option for her because she still had to complete her education degree. In hindsight, it was probably a good thing. I didn't feel that my heart was completely committed. I still thought about Lisa a lot.

It was around Christmas when Lisa called to tell me that she and Joe had gotten engaged. I was actually happy for her, because I wanted her to be happy, and I told her so. We had spoken occasionally in the preceding months and she knew I had been trying to strengthen my relationship with Jenny. I knew that her marriage to Joe was imminent.

But before long I found myself longing to be with Lisa again. I constantly thought about the laughs we had shared, the natural bond we'd had and the way I felt when we shared a bed. A few months later, I broke it off with Jenny and spent hours on the phone trying to talk Lisa out of marrying Joe and to convince her that we could make it work, that we were perfect for each other.

Conveniently, I was sent to Cleveland for a sales meeting, and I took the opportunity to go out on a limb. Lisa already had an engagement ring, so I proposed to her with a pair of diamond earrings. She wasn't married yet and there was no way in hell I was going to give up without a fight. She was constantly on my mind. I loved her. Unfortunately for Lisa, she was in love with two men. Yes, that *is* possible. Just ask her.

She thought about it. She cried about it. Nevertheless, the answer was no. Joe, she said, was "money in the bank," and that had nothing to do with financial comfort. She meant that he had been with her and true to her for years and she would be able to rely on him as a loving and faithful husband. I was the wild one. I was the one she couldn't count on. Besides, what would she tell her family?

I know what I would have told them: "I love Lisa."

Lisa got married to Joe. I agonized over that one. I was at the wedding.

(Since that time, Lisa has been divorced and re-married. She married Jim, another Lincoln guy, someone I like. Knowing that she was now with one of the good guys made it easier to swallow. When she eventually got pregnant, that finalized the deal. I got over her.)

While I was struggling with the whole love thing, athletics positively channeled my energies. As in the past, ice hockey became my team sport of choice. I played center for a C-league team in New Jersey comprised of, among others, a group of high school friends from the Somerset area: Jack Barr, Cliff Betron and Mike Tublin. They became my new circle of friends. We were members of The Express, a team randomly assembled by the inaugural league's administrators at the newly constructed Bridgewater Sports Arena. The team ended the season dead last the year I played for them. I felt I contributed in a positive way by centering a line, scoring a few goals and setting an example by hustling after the puck.

I couldn't skate nearly as well as I once had. This caused a certain level of frustration, but also provided an opportunity to challenge myself. I still loved to play the game, so the only option was to adapt and overcome. I worked at it and eventually got to the point where I could play an entire game without a blatant fall (falling for no particular reason whatsoever).

Early in my first season back on skates, I chased an opponent into the corner and, as I lost my balance, crashed into the boards, feet first. The prosthetic hit in such a way that it twisted off, folding forward at the knee. The referee's eyes popped out in disbelief. He was ignorant of my use of hardware and assumed that my knee had totally dislocated. I lay there chuckling. When he realized the deal, he said in frustrated relief, "You could've at least told me about that thing. I almost had a heart attack!"

My teammates were in hysterics. "Next game you'd better use more duct tape!" one of the guys jabbed. Mike Tublin's son Jake, who was five years old when he witnessed the fiasco, told his father that he didn't want to play ice hockey because his leg might fall off!

John Callahan, proprietor and prosthetist at the Center for Orthotics and Prosthetics in Union, New Jersey, was the first man to build me a specialty leg. I found his practice in the yellow pages and visited his facility to buy a couple of new woolen stump socks. We discussed ice hockey and he soon offered to build me a leg designed specifically for the sport. John was the official orthotist of the National Hockey League's New Jersey Devils; he had a passion for the game. He had wanted to build a designated skating prosthesis for quite some time but didn't have a qualified patient. I gladly obliged, volunteering as test amputee.

The simple prosthetic leg worked well. The benefits included less weight and better alignment. Eliminating the boot lessened the weight, directly improving agility. A standard skate blade was mounted to an aluminum plate. We tested several locations along the plate for mounting the ankle mechanism and pylon, the structural component between the socket and ankle, to give the greatest leverage with proper balance. These factors, combined with an improved suspension system, eliminated my reliance on duct tape, which in turn provided greater flexion at the knee. The sport became much more enjoyable and certainly less frustrating.

Solid performances on the ice led to my first newspaper coverage since high school. The local paper heard of my ability to play center for an able-bodied team and ran a two-page article, mostly photos. A public television station then aired a two-minute piece during their news program. I fortuitously scored a goal for my visual airwaves debut, but that footage didn't make the final cut.

In a game later that year, I scored another hat trick. That was big. Motivated by his earlier claim that I wouldn't be playing center anymore, I phoned my father to boast of the accomplishment before my skates had a chance to dry. I told him that I had just scored the second hat trick of my organized ice hockey career and the first on a prosthetic leg. He was nearly as proud of me as I was of myself.

I could play hockey and I could ski, but I still couldn't run. The foot absorbed too much energy and the suspension system worked insufficiently, which was the biggest problem. Duct tape or no duct tape, I could only take a dozen strides or so before the leg would loosen and "piston." Pistoning results from insufficient suspension where the residual limb slides in and out of the socket during each stride. The induced rubbing and abrasion leads to discomfort, blisters and miserable pain when repeatedly bearing full body weight.

Thirteen months after the amputation, I found the name and home phone number of Mike Joyce, a prosthetist in Queens, in my wallet. It was in my handwriting. I had no idea where that number had come from. I called to set up an appointment.

I made a trip to Advanced Prosthetics and Orthotics a week later. (Mike's practice has since moved to Manhassett, Long Island and has been renamed the Joyce Center.) Mike introduced himself and handed me a leg he had built for Dennis Oehler, one of the world's most successful amputee runners to date. Mike designed the leg for sprinting and nothing else, not even a fast-pace run. The carbon fiber socket was attached to a carbon fiber "foot." The pylon/ankle/foot was a thin strip of braided carbon fiber, about one quarter inch thick and three inches wide, that protruded from the socket and gently curved 90 degrees in a six-inch radius—somewhat of a J shape. Fastened to the forward part of the foot, which would constitute toes, was the sole of a sprinter's shoe, complete with spikes. The prosthesis amazed me. I knew I had found someone who could build the leg I so desperately wanted.

Now I faced the challenge of convincing my insurance company that I needed an athletic prosthetic leg to return me to the fitness level I had enjoyed before the accident. This task required patience and determination. My attempts, properly backed by formal letters from medical doctors and certified prosthetists, were shot down again and again. Another leg, the insurers claimed, was not medically necessary. I became very discouraged.

Mike assured me that one way or another he would get the underwriters to pay for a new leg. In the meantime, he would build it and worry about payment afterward.

Less than a month later, I had my new prosthesis. It was very different from the sprinting leg, and for good reason. The leg would function as both an everyday walking leg and one I could use for running and other sports. The Re-Flex VSP, by Flex-Foot, consisted of a vertical shock pylon that reduced the amount of jarring to my knee, hip and back, and also helped to smooth out the roll-over from heel to toe in walking stride. It also had a carbon fiber, energy-storing foot.

The socket, which incorporated a quality suspension system, was also considerably different. I learned there was more to socket building than molding the stump and creating a negative form. The "total contact socket" used more of the surface area of my stump to bear weight.

My first prosthetic leg was held in place by a neoprene sleeve. The tube-like sleeve extended from several inches below the top of the socket to several inches above it, making direct contact with the skin of my thigh. This was a very poor system for someone who enjoyed any significant level of activity, particularly with a relatively short stump like mine—five inches below the knee.

The new "3S" system (silicone suction socket) consisted of a custom-fit liner, made of a silicone injected cotton matrix, which, beginning inside-out, I would roll onto my stump to just over the knee. On the distal end of this sleeve was a pin about an inch long. The pin aligned with a hole in the bottom of the socket. As I placed my stump into the socket, the pin would enter the hole and ratchet into a receiving shuttle lock to a point where my leg was fully inserted. The intimacy of this custom sleeve, theoretically, allowed no air to enter, which greatly reduced pistoning.

A button was placed midway along the frame of the prosthesis for removal of the leg. Pushing the button released the ratchet from the pin, allowing me to remove my stump from the socket. I used the same system for my hockey leg.

I tested myself on the treadmill the day I received the new leg.

Starting at a slow trot for a few minutes, I speeded up to stride, then ran faster still until I almost couldn't keep up with the machine.

I was running!

I had not run in any appreciable sense in more than a year, and I ran nearly half a mile that day. Mike told me in a semi-serious tone that he would have me running a marathon within two years. I laughed. I had no intention or desire to go that distance. But I appreciated the notion that he would take me as far as I wanted to go.

When I had been running for three months, Mike asked if I wanted to take a stab at the National Amputee Track & Field Games held in Baltimore that summer. Because I was reluctant to compete (I was in no hurry to be humbled by the veteran runners), Mike had to convince me that I'd place well among the competition. With his encouragement, I jumped in, head first, and signed up for nearly every event. The meet included the 100- through 5,000-meter runs along with jumping and throwing events.

I had no experience with the shot put or discus, nor had I practiced these events before making the trip. It showed. In the pentathlon, the first event, I was seriously out-performed in the throwing disciplines. However, I finished both the 100- and 400-meter runs with reasonable times. In the end, I finished second in my first pentathlon—out of three competitors!

Later in the week I won the 1500-meter race; I had to beat one guy. The 1500 was considered a fairly long race for leg amputees, and most potential competitors were deterred for fear of stump problems. I soon learned why. Upon finishing the event, I removed my leg and discovered a large blister on the anterior distal tibia—the bottom of Stumpie. The resulting pain prevented me from taking part in any further competition that week.

This was the first of many running-related skin problems I would have to deal with. Very many. But it was also the beginning of something big. Very big.

For one thing, there was the dawning of a realization that I could affect others. Their outlook on life. Their ability to cope with losses similar to mine.

My first opportunity came when I helped another man adjust to life on a prosthetic leg.

Milton Gaylord had starred as a high school basketball player and had hoped one day to play in the NBA. Having come up short as a professional player out of college, Milton took a job teaching high school mathematics in inner city Newark, New Jersey—not the easiest assignment. And he shifted his competitive focus to the game of tennis.

Sometime around Milton's 35th birthday, the doctors diagnosed a cancerous tumor in the arch of his left foot. For two years, he battled localized radiation treatments, drugs and a lot of pain, and found himself bound to crutches. The doctors began to discuss amputation of his leg below the knee.

It was a tough choice: hope it heals or get rid of it and start over. Milton contacted me through the folks at the Joyce Center for an honest discussion about life on a peg-leg. We soon became friends. I had just begun my career as a reborn athlete and was excited about all the opportunities in front of me; I felt lucky to be able to show someone "the light." He saw that my prosthetic hadn't held me back, and that made him feel more comfortable with the idea of having one himself. Two months later, he had the operation. Four months later, he was playing tennis again. One year later, he was voted New Jersey High School Basketball Coach of the Year.

Milton helped me by letting me help him.

In the meantime, I needed help too, to pursue my own athletic ambitions. I began to seek sponsorship opportunities to help with travel, equipment and other race-related expenses. I felt that I was a marketing story waiting to happen.

I lived in Summit, New Jersey, at the time, so I approached the manager of Summit Bank to discuss a possible sponsorship. A marketing executive made the call and graciously offered to cover my expenses for the National Track & Field Games as well as the cost of some new ski equipment. She also contacted the mayor to boast of my accomplishments, which weren't anything more than playing hockey and doing well at the amputee track meet. A few months later, the city council presented me with a proclamation that declared November 4, 1994 as Paul Martin Day in the city of Summit. King for a Day! I loved it.

I was introduced to the sport of triathlon the following summer after picking up a triathlon magazine one day. I flipped through the pages and saw a photo of Cam Widoff crossing a finish line in a shirt that read "Will Race For Food." This simple statement impressed me—*triathlon must be a pretty hip sport.*

My desire to complete a triathlon grew after I heard about Jim MacLaren. At 290 pounds, Jim played defensive end for the Yale football team in the mid-80s. A collision with a Manhattan bus while riding his motorcycle led to the amputation of his left leg below the knee. The EMTs pronounced Jim dead, twice, en route to the hospital. Thankfully, he survived and went on to become a very competitive triathlete. (As of this writing, Jim holds below-knee amputee records in both the marathon—three hours, 15 minutes—and the Hawaiian Ironman Championship, the Superbowl of triathlon—10:42. An Ironman-distance triathlon consists of a 2.4-mile swim and a 112-mile bike ride followed by a 26.2-mile run. It's no walk in the park even for a healthy, able-bodied athlete.)

Jim's struggle expanded in 1993. While competing in a triathlon in Orange County, California, his bike, at full speed, broadsided a van that had illegally entered the course. Jim suffered a broken neck in the crash, rendering him quadriplegic. He now makes his way around in a motorized wheelchair, but his indomitable spirit is as mobile as ever.

Jim's accomplishments awed me. Up until that time, I considered a marathon an incredible feat to tackle with a prosthetic leg. But an Ironman? It sounded so extreme. Still, it was motivating to know that the list of possible achievements had no apparent end. Jim became a role model and gave me confidence to begin training for some shorter triathlons.

I decided to buy a mountain bike to begin training for my first triathlon. When I picked up the bike I had ordered from the Cosmic Wheel in Ridgefield, New Jersey, I met Dr. Rob DeStefano, a chiropractor in nearby Lodi. Dr. DeStefano was talking about his own Hawaiian Ironman experience with the shop's proprietor. I stuck my nose into the conversation, telling Dr. Rob of my triathlon ambitions, and mentioning Jim MacLaren. Rob was familiar with him from races they had both competed in on the Big Island of Hawaii. Without hesitation, he agreed to help me get started in the sport.

Three days later, thieves stole the new bike off the rack of my car in broad daylight from outside my house in Weehawken. They cut the rack's nylon straps with scissors they left by my rear tire, next to the beat-up old banana seat bike they no longer needed now that they had mine.

I suspected the perpetrators might be some of the less respectful youths from nearby Union City, so I drove down the main drag thinking they might be mindless enough to strut around town with my bike. Sure enough, a half dozen young teens were hanging out on a street corner, with my bike and another one that I imagined belonged to someone else. In my white shirt and tie, I approached the group. One of the bigger kids took a swig out of my water bottle. I grabbed the bottle from his hand as he drank from it and said, in a low-key, confident voice, "I'm taking my bike back." They muttered some things I did not understand. Then the largest member of the gang asked, "Who are you?"

"I'm taking my fucking bike back!" I repeated. I grabbed it, threw it over my shoulder and walked away...nervously, wondering if they would try to jump me from behind or throw a knife at me before I got into my car. But they didn't. As I drove off, they flipped me the bird and one of them yelled, "Go fuck yourself!"

Two days later my car window was smashed and my radio and CD changer were stolen.

A week later I met Dr. Rob at the Hackensack YMCA for a swim lesson. He chuckled when I demonstrated my technique. One lap, a mere fifty yards, left me huffin' and puffin'. He pointed out the gross errors, including a horribly inefficient and hastened stroke, a misaligned body and an improper kick. But by the end of the month, swimming two to three days a week, my ability improved, I quadrupled in distance and nearly doubled in speed.

Dr. Rob then set me up with a 12-week program to help me complete my first sprint triathlon. Sprint races vary in distance but typically involve a half-mile swim, a 10- to 15-mile bike ride, and a three- to five-mile run. I continued to swim at the Hackensack YMCA and usually ran and cycled on the streets near Weehawken. Central Park was only a 20-minute commute on any given weekend. I spent most Saturday and Sunday afternoons there getting ready for my first race.

I found the perfect event to test my new abilities in my hometown of Gardner. By race day, my swimming technique was still weak, so I used a pull buoy to conserve energy. Flotation devices are usually not allowed in triathlon, but the sympathetic race director let me use one.

The bike section felt good, and I passed several competitors along the way, including a high school buddy who was cycling for a relay team. Stomach cramps late in the race made for a difficult run, but once the pain subsided I reeled in a few runners who had previously passed me. In the finish line sprint, I matched a competitor along the last 50 meters before he got the best of me. My grandmother, aunt and uncle, and some friends were there to cheer me through the finish. I placed 44th out of over 100 triathletes. I felt pretty damn good—despite a blistered Stumpie.

I had trained primarily for the run, which is the toughest discipline for an amputee. My running improved throughout that summer in both distance and speed. Mike and his head prosthetist, Erik Shaffer, made continual socket adjustments to help me run with less pain. "Pain free" running, I have discovered, may very well remain theoretical. (Erik has recently gone out on his own and opened A Step Ahead Prosthetics and

Orthotics on Long Island.)

In the 18 months since I first ran on Mike's treadmill, I had competed on a national level in track and field, and had completed my first triathlon. I was mentally prepared for my next challenge: the 1995 National Amputee Track & Field Games being held in Boston at the MIT athletic facilities in June.

I was running three or four days a week; Stumpie couldn't handle any more than that. I would run on the Hoboken High School track a couple of times a week and a day or two on the road. I was also making many trips to the prosthetic shop to try to find an answer to my blistering problems. We were making gradual progress.

My duties at work lost their priority. I was putting all my creative energy into training. That was all that mattered to me. And the training began to pay off.

In Boston, I set a new national 1500-meter record with a time of 5:20:88. I also ran the 400-meter and managed both a second place finish and a personal record time of 64.95 seconds, not particularly fast. In the 100-meter race, not having yet mastered my new sprinting leg, I tripped on the prosthesis right out of the starting blocks, but still managed to set another personal best of 13.93 seconds. Again, not too fast. I didn't even qualify for the final heat of six runners. Still, I was developing a passion for mastering the run.

For the remainder of the summer I focused on the race Mike Joyce had predicted less than two years before: the New York City Marathon. A newly found friend became a motivator and mentor: Kathy Holmes, who was a member of the Somerset circle of friends I had entered by way of the ice hockey team and who had run the race the previous year, 1994, dared me to match her courage. The seeds of 26.2 miles of self-induced punishment were sown. To help guide my training she bought me a book for my birthday, *Making the Marathon Your Event,* by Richard Benyo.

Distance running was teaching me a great deal about prosthetic equipment. The more I ran, the more often I had to make the two-hour trip to the leg shop. I discovered that skin breakdown problems were caused not only by pistoning but also by the changing shape of my stump. Training resulted in a loss of body fat, even in Stumpie. This meant a change in shape and socket fit.

Suspension was a huge problem now that I was running the longer miles. I found a partial solution in a clear silicone liner that Erik thought we should try. The primary suspension problem was the introduction of air into the 3S, eliminating the intimate vacuum fit and causing enough pistoning to create abrasions and blistering. I wore an off-the-shelf silicone liner—a tube with a closed, cupped distal end—over my 3S. We cut a hole in the end for my pin to protrude to the shuttle lock. Its flexibility allowed for a tight fit up through my mid-thigh, thus preventing air from entering the 3S while still allowing sufficient flexion at the knee; this key innovation would contribute to my early distance running success.

Marathon day: November 12, 1995—cold and rainy, 29 degrees Fahrenheit at the start. Sixty-mile per hour winds blew across the Verrazano Bridge, the first quarter mile of the marathon. I was dressed in mid-thigh Spandex shorts, a cotton T-shirt, nylon shell, official John Hancock cotton race hat and cotton gloves. Jurassic runwear but, hey, I was a rookie.

My hockey buddy, Jack Barr, had also accepted Kathy's challenge. He joined me for the race along with Joan Nevin, a volunteer from Achilles Track Club. I would be running the race as a member of a club that had been founded to promote physically challenged runners and wheelers.

The three of us took our own sweet time preparing for the start of the race and, as a result, ended up in the back of the pack…of 27,500 runners! The organizers had recommended self-seeding, whereby a competitor places him/herself within the masses according to his/her anticipated race pace. We failed miserably in this regard. We reached the start line 20 minutes after the gun fired.

Plastic bags by the hundreds, which athletes donned to stay dry while waiting for the gun to fire, blew by and got entangled in many racers' legs, causing some to stumble and fall. We managed nine-minute miles for the first part of the race by bobbing and weaving our way through the melee. By Mile 4 we increased our speed to eight-and-a-half-minute miles, then to eight-minute miles by Mile 7. As I ran, the constant pounding and slightly less than perfect socket fit inhibited circulation, causing increasingly intolerable pain. At Mile 8, I had to pull over to remove the leg to restore desperately needed blood flow. The pain forced me to remove the leg more and more frequently as the race progressed.

At each pit stop, the same pair of women passed us. We would return to battle to regain the lead, each of us making some type of "you again" comment. (One of the women researched my name and contact information through Achilles after the race and wrote weeks later, praising my efforts. In fact, Sarina Glaser kept up the correspondence and remained a self-proclaimed "Number One Fan" for quite some time.)

We backed off to an eight-and-a-half-minute pace for the next eight miles, until we reached the Queensboro Bridge. Across the East River, the athletes were treated to the energizing roar of the crowd on First Avenue. The five-person-deep crowd on either side of the street stretched for more than a mile. Kathy, my sister Paty, and some other friends were planning to meet us at the northwest corner of 59th Street. Like every other runner who had friends and family in the crowd, I looked forward to seeing a familiar face. My body started to hurt and my leg pain became more and more of a problem. Seeing them would hopefully provide renewed energy.

Then there they were—smiling and cheering us on. Paty even carried a sign: "Go Paul from Gardner, Mass!" I'm pretty sure she just wanted to get the attention of the TV crew and get on the tube. We stopped and chatted a bit before I gave each of them a reassuring hug to let them know that all was fine.

The run up First Avenue was fabulous. Millions of people were cheering for their friends and family members as well as for total strangers. We heard, "Go Achilles!"—the official cheer for any challenged runner—over and over again. In classic rookie fashion, Joan and I had each written, "Go

Paul" on our shirts to spark a bit of encouragement from the spectators. It actually worked.

The race crossed the East River again, this time eastbound, on the Willis Avenue Bridge. There, at Mile 18, I hit the infamous "Wall." This unwelcome threshold is reached when the muscle glycogen stores, then blood glucose, become so depleted that further energy must be supplied through food intake. Otherwise, muscles will begin to cannibalize and the central nervous system will experience severe fatigue. Jack humbly held himself back. Joan, too, could have maintained a quicker pace but chose to hang back with us. The Wall slowed our troop of three from what had been a nine-minute pace to a struggling 12-minute pace.

It was in this section of the race that I learned how wondrous an orange slice can be, how splendid its juices running down my throat can feel, how much energy one slice can provide. The sustenance came from the volunteer aid stations every mile along the course. Each pit was staffed by 20 to 25 God-sent individuals distributing water, Gatorade, oranges, bananas and energy bars.

Until then, the crowds had graced us with desperately needed enthusiasm and encouragement, but on the other side of the bridge in the Bronx, the sidelines were considerably thinner than they had been on Manhattan Island.

On the streets of this northernmost New York City borough, the race took a very hard right turn, causing a bottleneck in the flow of runners. Jack pulled off to get a banana and that was the last I saw of him for the remainder of the race. He had a more aggressive goal than I did, so I was relieved that I was no longer holding him back.

From the Bronx, we headed south onto Manhattan Island and into Harlem, at approximately Mile 20. By then, Stumpie was bummin' hard and I had to stop at least once every mile. I stopped at one park bench for nearly two minutes—two minutes that passed much too quickly. Then Joan and I went on. The crowds became thinner still and the surrounding athletes thinned also. It became a mental feat just to keep moving.

Miles 20 through 23, the toughest of the day, drilled down Fifth Avenue through Harlem. This was an interesting section of the race, highlighted by the wonderfully welcomed smiles from the elderly ladies and little kids who probably witnessed the rite annually. In the heart of that infamous part of town, I consoled myself with the knowledge that I had less than 10 kilometers to go, a standard run on any other day. But it wasn't any other day. I was nearing the end of my first marathon, and Stumpie was killing me!

The inspiration to keep moving actually came from the other runners. All around me I could see that their legs were burning and their feet were getting heavy—but they were still running.

Paty and the others had planned to meet us again at the entrance to Central Park at Fifth Avenue and 102nd Street. That corner would be a natural energy boost for all the competitors. The park marked the beginning of the end, and all the spectators from First Avenue had meandered west to catch the big finish. I didn't see my friends where they said they would be and I was a bit bummed. *Had I missed them? Were they not expecting us so early?*

I stayed focused on finding them to provide both a goal, as I was sure to pull over and rest for a bit before proceeding, and a distraction from the extreme discomfort I was experiencing. Just past Mile 24, I heard them all hollering my name as Joan and I came into view. Paty kept waving her big, happy sign. They were all glad to see me upright and likely to finish. I plodded along at nearly an 11-minute-mile pace. We'd have just two more miles to go when we got back into the pack.

I pulled off the road and sat on a wall with Paty and Kathy. I removed not just my leg but also the liner and 3S. Stumpie was so tender. Regardless, we laughed and cheered and began a premature celebration. Although I was in no hurry to put that damned leg back on, I re-donned the equipment, post-hug, and pulled myself together to get out there for the last of the punishment.

With only minutes left in the struggle, my psyche strengthened and I began to feel wonderful. The pace picked up as we passed a slew of runners through the southern progression of the park. We briefly ran along the westbound half-mile stretch of Central Park South, the section of 59th Street adjacent to the southern edge of the park. I became incredibly energized. I was running at nearly a seven-minute-mile pace! I had to bark, "On your left!" time and again to clear a path. When we turned north back into the park, we had just 0.2 miles left. The crowd had been cheering incessantly since our entrance at Mile 23. The finish line bleacher seats came into view. *Beautiful...*

There it was, the finish line of the New York City Marathon. I kicked it in for an honorable finish, remembering Kathy's advice: "Make sure no one's around you when you get to within 30 feet of the finish line and put your arms up in victory. You'll get a great finish line photo." I slowed it up to a standstill until the immediate crowd surrounding me dispersed. Then I howled and threw my arms toward the sky and proceeded at a trot across the white line. Despite coming up 30 minutes short of my goal, a victorious feeling overwhelmed me from the inside out. And the finish line photo was perfect.

I received my finisher's medal and, like everyone else, plodded along in euphoric discomfort toward the family and friends meeting place *another three quarters of a mile through the park!* On the way, a park bench lawlessly invited me over for a reflective moment. I ignored the "No Crossing" tape and accepted the invitation.

Joan asked if I was okay and I told her that I just needed to be alone for a short while. When she had gone, I sat and cried for a good five minutes. A race volunteer approached and put her arm around me for comfort. I assured her that I couldn't be happier. She smiled and left me to my thoughts.

I had just completed a marathon—in New York City. It was an accomplishment I had never considered pursuing in my 10-toed days. The finish line, earned through hard work and determination, taught me a lesson: at that moment I knew that anything I wanted to do, in any field, for any reason, was possible. If I dedicated myself to any reasonable goal, I could ultimately achieve it.

It occurred to me then that I was not only "as good" as I had been before the amputation; I was better. This accomplishment would be the launch pad to a future of unrestricted possibilities.

But the first step, no trivial task, was to get off that bench! In those few minutes my legs and back had stiffened terribly, but I had to get to the meeting place to find the others. I hobbled for nearly 20 minutes to the Great Lawn to find them all there waiting for me, even Jack. Hugs and high-fives ensued. So much pain, so much joy. Funny how that works. It was clearly time to celebrate. Time for a good meal and a good beer, both well deserved. We decided on an Irish bar on First Avenue, near Kathy's place.

With so many people in the city for the race, it was impossible to hail a cab or even get on a bus. As we debated various means of transportation—walking was not an option for me at this point—a limousine pulled up and dropped off a few people.

"Hey!" (When the situation calls for it, and this one did, I have no qualms about using my unique status to my advantage.) "I just ran the marathon on this leg and it's killing me! Any chance you can get us to First Avenue?"

"Get in."

"Yahoo!"

The closest the driver could take us was the Plaza Hotel on the southeastern corner of Central Park (59th Street and Fifth Avenue). The limo door opened and the doorman took one look at our motley crew and walked away. We laughed, got out, and were blessed with a cab just as soon as the stretched Town Car pulled away.

An amazing thing happened when we got to the tavern. Still in a state of numbed misery, I gimped up to the doorway and took in the sight of a hundred happy, marathon-celebrating fanatics. A wonderful sight. Not until an hour later did I realize that the pain was gone! Just by putting myself in the company of all these happy people—and being quite content myself—I helped my decrepit, throbbing body to stop hurting.

In the meantime, a high-strung group noticed that Jack and I were still sporting our medals and race numbers.

"Congratulations!" one exclaimed. I pulled up my pant leg, obnoxiously bragging, and showed them the hardware. The boys howled. One commented, "Holy shit! We saw you in Central Park, man!" To show their appreciation, they kept the beer flowing, and the party raged on until midnight. This was, without a doubt, the best mood I had ever been in for any given eight-hour period. So I did what seemed appropriate. I called my mom.

The next day I discovered that my car had been towed…after someone broke into it. They got away with a couple of coats, my driving gloves, a half-eaten pack of Rolaids and the remote to my car stereo. The perpetrator apparently had no use for my cell phone or the stereo itself. Probably a homeless person—I'm glad he or she got some warm clothing out of the deal.

The break-in hardly fazed me. My leg hurt too much that morning—and my heart felt too good—for anything to really be a problem. Besides, who needs a remote to the car stereo?

Skiing, Triathlon and
My Grandparents

My quest for a ski racing career had begun at New Jersey's Mount Vernon ski area, in the winter of 1995, before the marathon. Pat Hubner, the director of the resort's competitive program, allowed me to train— well, learn to ski—with his junior race team on weeknights, in the lights, in the rain and slush…in New Jersey.

Soon after I joined the program, a small sore on Stumpie, caused by my running, trapped a bacteria that caused a serious cellulitis infection. The environment inside a 3S is warm and moist—a prime single-cell organism breeding ground. The infection worked its way down to the bone and required emergency outpatient surgery to prevent contamination of the bone itself, as well as, yikes, further amputation. A small skin graft was taken from my left hip to expedite healing while the entire process kept me from walking for six weeks.

By the time I could ski again the race season was well underway. To begin again in the middle of the competitive season seemed futile; I would just have to try again next year. For the next couple of months, I put in as many miles as I could on skis to become comfortable on the new equipment.

Erik and Mike at the Joyce Center had built me a ski-specific prosthesis. This leg attached directly to the binding, bypassing the need for a boot. We used only the sole of a ski boot, attaching it directly to a standard Flex-Foot walking pylon. I looked forward to the benefits the light-weight prosthetic would provide when, later that season, a few friends and I headed to Colorado for a week-long ski trip.

On the first morning on the snowy slopes of Breckenridge, I attacked a mogul field in wild abandon and snapped the pylon near the ankle. The entire county must have heard the resulting expletives. The responsiveness and proper alignment I had so enthusiastically looked forward to suddenly became two distinct, sharply frayed pieces of carbon fiber.

Determined not to let this misfortune ruin my vacation, I decided to challenge myself on a single ski. I played on one ski—single-tracked—for the rest of the day. There were numerous crashes, of course. Nothing new.

The next day I tested the turns using my walking leg…for about an hour. A crash loosened the connection in the middle of my prosthesis where the pylon meets the socket. I lay down on my right side on a semi-steep slope with my skis parallel—and then glanced down to see that the skis were pointing in opposite directions. Damn it!

A concerned skier approached to see if I needed any assistance. His eyes bugged, just as the hockey referee's once had, when he saw what he assumed to be a severely dislocated left knee. He began to pant, struggling for a breath.

"Not to worry, Bud, it's artificial," I said as I knocked on the plastic socket. The man didn't say another word. He skied away in a daze, shaking his head.

The walking-leg repair turned out to be simple and I continued to abuse myself for a few more days.

I enjoyed the people, the vistas and the snow quality so much in Colorado that I gave my boss my six-month notice when I returned to New Jersey. I told Charlie that I would be leaving for the Rocky Mountain State in early December to pursue a spot on the U.S. Disabled Alpine Ski Team, to compete in Nagano, Japan, at the 1998 Winter Paralympic Games.

Frankly, I knew next to nothing about ski racing or about the U.S. Disabled Alpine Ski Team—except that I wanted to be a member. I was done selling welding machines to guys who didn't want me to sell them welding machines.

Every week for the next few months, Charlie questioned me on my decision. You can call it a blessing or a curse, because sometimes it gets me into trouble, but once I get something in my head, it's almost impossible to get it out. The fact was, I wanted to continue my progress on the track and pursue competition at the upcoming 1996 Summer Paralympic Games in Atlanta, too. I found the prospect of representing my country in both summer and winter competition extremely compelling.

I selected Winter Park, Colorado as the best location for training, both as a skier and a runner. I had visited Winter Park in 1994 with members of the Lincoln sales staff. A company-wide sales incentive awarded either a golf or ski trip to promote a new line of plasma cutters. (We're not talking blood here, but super-charged electric current capable of cutting any type of metal.) The top three offices and top 10 individuals, in terms of units sold, took the prize. By popular vote, a four-day excursion to Winter Park Ski Resort was chosen over the links. I had arrived at the New York office a week before the contest ended and had not actually sold a single machine, but thanks to the efforts of my office counterparts, I was a winner.

We were only allowed four hours a day to ski, snowmobile, snowshoe or relax because our primary retreat focus was sales training, general brown-nosing and other corporate activities. I did find enough time to gather information about the National Sports Center for the Disabled (NSCD), located at the base of the mountain. Their competitive program offered a five-day per week, full-time training schedule. On-snow training, video analysis and the travel/race schedule meant a full-time commitment. No disabled ski program in the country could compare, so this was the obvious choice for me to fast track my way into the sport.

I arrived in Winter Park on December 2, 1995, another new and exciting beginning. This commencement had a very shaky business plan. I had the utmost confidence in my athletic potential, but obtaining the necessary funds to sustain such an undertaking was a bit daunting. I had walked away from a promising career with a comfortable salary—$52,000 a year with the bonus. I had given it all up for the chance to passionately pursue whatever life had to offer.

Friends and family expressed various points of view: "You're crazy! You're just gonna throw away your college education?" "Good for you, Paul. I wish I could do that." "How do you know you're going to like ski racing?"

I took a leap of faith, believing everything would be fine. Really, what's the worst thing that could happen? I'd go back to work at something I might actually enjoy?

At times I wondered if I was quitting the "real world" because I couldn't handle it. The daily grind, which so many millions of people go through for the sake of their futures and families, was difficult and unsatisfying—surprise, surprise. Before resigning from my position with Lincoln, I had realized that, generally speaking, I was a happy individual and I should stop doing the things that make me unhappy. One of those things was sacrificing my time and passions for the sake of a paycheck. I wondered if the continuous drive toward corporate success would actually mean "success." If I did become CEO of the company, would that guarantee happiness?

Still, it took a great deal of effort not to let my ego convince me that the material things I could earn would equal success. I had just bought a new car—a 1995 Saturn SLII, fully loaded. At least for a day, that new car felt, to me, like success. (This same car would soon run out of gas at 4:45 p.m. on a Friday afternoon exiting New York City's Lincoln tunnel. I don't think I'll ever again see that many middle fingers in a 15-minute period.) The fact that I was making enough money to buy a new car seemed to indicate that I was doing something right. Or so I thought. I was 28 years old. People get married and have kids at that age. They don't suddenly chase Olympic honors. John Stropki at Lincoln headquarters questioned my decision to pursue full-time athletics at such a late age, practically over-the-hill. He had expected great things from me for the company.

But I expected much more meaningful things of myself. I craved a state of self-realization—the knowledge that the life I lead is the right one for me.

Before committing to a life of shameless self-promotion, I visited my grandmother, whom we French-Canadians call Mémère, to seek her advice. I told her that I wanted to quit my job, a job that paid more money than she and Pépère ever made combined, to be a ski racer.

Money, she told me, was never much of a concern to her. She could see it wasn't making me happy, either. "You don't want to be my age and say, 'What if?' You better pack your bags," she said.

Wise words from a wise woman. That sealed it.

She also told me that day what being "rich" meant to her: she showed me a letter she had written to a friend after a weekend together in New York City.

March 1966

What I think being rich means.

Is having a friend think enough of me to invite me to her house for a weekend. I could have gone to the best hotel in New York and pay—I would have been alone.

Is having her sister greet me at the door and making me feel welcome in her home. Instead of a strange bellhop at the hotel.

Is sitting at her table and eating food prepared especially for me, while Larry, her nephew, entertained us on the piano. Instead of eating alone in a famous restaurant.

Is having a friend think enough of me to take a day off to take me sight-seeing in New York City. Instead of taking a tour of the city alone with no one to talk to.

Is having been poor enough to have to rip up old clothes to be able to dress my family by sewing them up into wearable clothes and learning a trade and developing a skill that has made me able to design clothes to compete with Dior, Bianchini, and the like. And being able to show my appreciation by fashioning a coat especially for Jim. Instead of being rich, going to college and getting a diploma and never having met a friend like you at 322 Waldo Street.

Thanks for a wonderful weekend.
Albina

Mémère's grounded attitude about simplicity and happiness gave me all the gumption I needed to put my professional career on hold. (Mémère is one of few people in this world I feel honored to spend time with. She even has a credit to her name at the Smithsonian Institute, in an exhibit on cultural cuisine. Her recipe for *les ployes*—pronounced "plugs," French-Canadian buckwheat pancakes and the breakfast of my predecessors for centuries—earned a timeless entry in those halls.) With Mémère's blessing, I put what little furniture I owned into storage, packed up the car and drove to Colorado.

When I arrived, I went straight to Boulder to check out the house my father built, which was adjacent to the one I destroyed, to stir up some pleasant memories. There was a young boy at home, 13 years old, who was foolish enough to let me in. I walked around the entire house, taking pictures to send back to Mom. I was in the master bedroom backing up to get the whole room when I bumped into the nightstand where a Madonna with Child tottered, then, in slow motion, fell and smashed into pieces before our eyes.

The boy looked at me, bug-eyed and horrified. I gave him the nine bucks I had in my pocket, said I was sorry and bolted.

I was forced to trade in the Saturn that I had owned for less than a year for an '85 Honda Prelude; I no longer had the means to make $408 monthly payments. I even lost a couple of thousand dollars on the deal, but I got over it. In the end, I came to love the Prelude. With her coat hanger door handle and personally-customized front bumper, she had character.

I had a new home in Colorado, an environment unlike any other. That apartment, my first solo habitat, was a tiny one-bedroom unit on the eastern side of the Fraser Valley, with a majestic view of Byer's Peak. Each morning presented a new glimpse of beauty. The Continental Divide, just a few miles behind me, radiated with alpenglow on most evenings, and a stunning pinkish light shone across the valley's eastern peaks at sunset. As in Breckenridge, the people were friendly and, with 350 inches of snow each season, world-class ski conditions were plentiful.

It became evident on my first day of training with the Winter Park Disabled Ski Team that I knew very little about the finer points of skiing. Danny Pufpaff, the head coach, evaluated me that morning: "You ski like a pig on roller skates!" he said. Dan was good for an honest attempt at humor. Once in a while, he even made someone laugh.

After only three days of training, with one day actually spent in race gates, our team departed for Breckenridge to participate in the ITT Hartford Ski Spectacular giant slalom event, traditionally the first race of the season. The race came at the end of a week-long camp of recreational and competitive ski lessons for individuals with all types of disabilities. The U.S. Disabled Ski Team was there, along with some members of the New Zealand Team, most of whom trained at Winter Park. One member of the Kiwi team and perhaps the best BK (below knee) skier of all time, Patrick Cooper, clocked 1:03 on the course; I finished in 1:33. My expectations were high, but it became clear that day—to me and everyone else—that I had a long way to go.

That was fine with me. I had until March of 1998, two full years before the Paralympics, to acquire the skills of an alpine ski racer.

Improvements came in leaps and bounds throughout the first season as I was taught the gross necessities of alpine ski racing theory: the proper line to ski and the proper technique in each of the four events—downhill, super giant slalom, giant slalom and slalom. But I had not expected that the proper care of race skis would be so difficult; tuning and maintenance play such a vital role in achieving maximum speed. It didn't take long for me to realize what a pain in the butt it is to keep four pairs of race skis, along with two pairs of training skis, in prime condition.

Without a doubt, I cherished my latest occupation, skiing all day, five days a week.

The team enjoyed having me as a member—not because of my personality, or my infectious determination, or my camaraderie, but solely due to my self-destructive entertainment value. I brought the same lack of concern for personal safety to the racecourse that I had carried with me as a recreational skier, and, yes, arguably, as a driver. I had a knack for consistently building up lots of speed and crashing in what would not be considered the classic "yard sale" but more of a "flea market." (The popular phrase "yard sale" is derived from the various pieces of equipment and clothing that often remain strewn across the trail after a crash as if on display for retail purposes.)

I bent, broke or trashed more skis in my short-lived career than any other racer I knew. Not to mention broken poles, goggles and, of course, a few bones.

In my first year, when I had so much to learn, the U.S. Team staff seemed to pay little attention to me. I wasn't gravely concerned because there was only one national team member in my category, Jim Lagerstrom, and he was debating retirement and no longer trained full time. We raced each other only once that year, near the end of the season, when he beat me by a few seconds in a super-G race. Without any true competition for a Paralympic slot, it appeared that the only hurdle I had to overcome was myself. If I stuck with it, I'd be rewarded with a trip to Nagano.

I reached the podium before the season's end with a bronze medal in the giant slalom of the Canadian Nationals, in Kimberly, British Columbia. My coaches began to see promise. The encouragement I received after that, and the potential I saw in myself, were enough to keep me excited for the following season. The prospect of competing in Japan was as appealing as ever. The first few rungs of the ladder were now below me, some broken and some skipped. Most important, I was enjoying my new life as an athlete.

Toward the end of my rookie ski season my mind began to drift toward summer competition. The Atlanta Paralympics were in a few months and I intended to compete on the track. I had yet to prove myself as a sprinter, so the only hope I had was the quasi-distance 400-meter event. This event is considered more of a sprint in two-legged circles, but it was the longest race the International Paralympic Committee (IPC) offered to lower-extremity amputees. (Since that time we have seen the addition of the 400- and 800-meter runs at the 2000 Sydney Games.)

Beginning in mid-March, I trained twice a week with the University of Colorado's track team in Boulder and a couple of days in Winter Park. My short-term goal was to break 60 seconds in the 400 before the Paralympic trials in May. Fresh off of skis, I was barely cracking 70 seconds on the indoor track. Obviously, I had work to do and not much time to do it. Just a few weeks into this transition, with little improvement yet seen, I received word that the 400-meter would not be run in Atlanta. The IPC reasoned that there were too few BK amputees in contention to stage the race. With so many different disabilities, the number of individual events becomes overwhelming, so the IPC was looking to cut down. Those events with the fewest entrants were eliminated.

Now that my summer's intentions were eliminated, I decided to travel to Hilton Head, South Carolina to spend some time with my father and play a little golf. He played; I hacked. (One of his friends, an older guy named Frank, would tell me a couple of years later that my visit had a long-term impact on his golf game. He had been complaining of back pain to his foursome when suddenly he thought of me. He confessed that he immediately found himself appreciating the round, remembering the day he had played with my father and me. Frank realized that he was still able to walk the course on two God-given legs and had little to fuss about. Somehow, two years later and 2,000 miles away, I helped Frank enjoy a game of golf. That's the kind of stuff that motivates me to keep doing what I do.)

While in Hilton Head, I did some fund-raising (shameless self-promoting), and I dared to sail Dad's boat again.

I should have known better. The mast line broke due to corrosion, and the mainsail came down on my shipmate, a woman I was hoping to impress with my finely-tuned marine skills. Luckily, we hadn't gotten too far. We had just left the dock and at that precise moment I hung up the boat on an oyster bed.

It was a fun two weeks. Dad's girlfriend Lillian was a spectacular chef.

But the days with Dad, spent enjoying each other's company and strengthening our friendship, were not typical.

By mid-June I was back in beautiful Winter Park, relishing its splendid summertime setting. The lack of humidity in this 9,000-feet-above-sea-level town, along with the consistently blue skies, made for a remarkably pleasant season. June was a bit soggy and September brought the cold, but July and August were fabulous. The locals claim that the summers keep them there. For both fitness and focus, I went back to Winter Park to train in the various disciplines of triathlon.

For good reason, the area is known as "Colorado's Favorite Mountain Biking Resort." Grand County contained only one stop light at the time. The Fraser Valley hosts most of the county's 600 miles of mountain bike trails. Other activities, like hiking, trail running, kayaking and white water rafting, occupy the lives of most residents.

I took a job framing houses for the good wages and rewarding practical experience. It felt good to work with my hands again—and the money was good—but athletic training remained my focus. I biked or ran for an hour or so after work most days, and most mornings I swam at the YMCA of the Rockies in nearby Tabernash. Tabernash was a few miles north of my home in Fraser, where most locals resided, and a mile down the road from Winter Park.

The job only lasted a few weeks, because my leg was too banged up to handle working on it all day, all because of snowboarding.

I had made my snowboarding debut a couple of months earlier at the end of the competitive season. Having spent 120 days that winter on the slopes, picking up this new sport was relatively easy. I had no problem linking turns and popping a little air here and there. On what ended up to be my final run on the first day, the socket of my walking leg broke completely in two when I came to an easy stop.

The duplicated socket I received a week later, via UPS, did not turn out to be nearly as "duplicate" as I had hoped. The local prosthetist I went to for adjustments wasn't worth his salt either. The ill-fitting socket made working on my feet all day framing houses a literal pain. It also tested my desire to run.

I opted to leave the job and limit the time I spent aggravating Stumpie to focus on the reason I moved to Colorado in the first place—to be an athlete, and to have a chance to travel to Atlanta for the Paralympic Games. Late in the summer, I went off to help one of my sponsors, even though I couldn't race.

MedLogic, my first real sponsor, had a booth set up in Atlanta at the Abilities Expo. The expo featured various products marketed to the disabled population—nearly 45,000,000 strong in the U.S. alone. MedLogic manufactured a product called SuperSkin (now called LiquiShield), which I used in my marathon training to help battle skin breakdown, the main cause of leg amputee debilitation. The company also assisted with race-related travel expenses and invited me to Atlanta to work their booth as a testimonial to the product.

In Atlanta, I was extremely envious of my friends who were there to compete. To feed my competitive hunger, I participated in a suburban sprint triathlon on the weekend. Prosthetic problems led to a lack of training, a slow race and a terribly painful run. Dad made the trip from nearby Hilton Head and witnessed not only my race but also the blood that dripped out of my liner when I doffed it just across the finish line.

Soon after, I flew to New York to have my socket completely rebuilt. After that, the pain subsided, relatively speaking, and I began to run again.

Around this time I responded to an offer from a hometown friend and fellow Frenchman, Phil LeClair. He was working for the Balance Bar Company and suggested I sample their meal replacement bars based on Dr. Barry Sear's "Zone Diet": 40 percent carbohydrates, 30 percent protein, and 30 percent fat measured as a percentage of total calories (a.k.a. the 40-30-30 diet). I called him for more information and, as requested, sent Balance Bar an athletic résumé. The product they sent me came with company logo T-shirts and a detailed media incentive contract that offered cash bonuses for various company exposure opportunities:

newspaper, magazine and television coverage in local, regional and national capacities. The company paid various amounts for logo exposure and/or company mention within the text or broadcast, depending on the media's volume of subscribers or viewers.

In September, a few weeks after signing with Balance Bar, I competed in a sprint triathlon in Glenwood Springs, Colorado. To test the contract's potential, I called up the local paper to inform them that an amputee triathlete would be competing in that weekend's race. The day after the race, I was pictured on the paper's front page sporting a Balance Bar singlet. I had also mentioned the company in the article…and was paid $400! It might not seem like much, but for an athlete living a frugal existence, this incentive program became the basis of my income and paved the way for my career as a "professional athlete."

Early in October I traveled to warm and sunny San Diego, California to compete in a series of triathlons at the invitation of Shawn Brown, an oversized BK amputee and discus world record holder. He invited me to stay at his place for a few weeks and take part in a couple of races with him and his girlfriend, Allison Pittman, an above-knee (AK) amputee and Paralympic gold medal-winning swimmer.

The first race, the Superfrog Triathlon, took place on the island of Coronado at the Navy SEAL training facility. The second, the San Diego Triathlon Challenge, was held in beautiful La Jolla. Both races were half Ironman distance (1.2 mile swim, 56 mile bike, and 13.1 mile run). The three of us assembled a relay team for each: Allison swam, Shawn cycled and I ran.

While Allison out-swam nearly the entire field, the Superfrog was super tough for Shawn and me. He hammered through the exhausting bike ride in reasonable time before handing me the baton.

The spirit-busting run course was comprised of six 2.2-mile loops. One half of this loop was on the beach, and half of the beach portion was on soft sand. I discovered that running in soft beach sand with a prosthetic leg is a miserable assignment. The toe sank into the soft medium, absorbing the energy otherwise used for forward progress and causing inappropriate weight bearing on areas not willing to accept it. Still, my goal for the day was a two-hour run and I stayed focused on that during the entire race.

I arrived at the finish line two hours and two minutes later, good enough for me. The real down side was my inability to walk for three days because Stumpie lost nearly six square inches of skin from various areas. Along with the pride that comes from conquering any tough challenge, I left Coronado a bit wiser about the challenges of running on a prosthetic leg.

With three weeks to go before the San Diego Triathlon Challenge, I found two nearby races to fill the weekends: the Mission Bay Triathlon, considered the first organized triathlon, and the Human Race Triathlon in Newport Beach, both sprint distance events. Stumpie was healed enough for me to compete in each event's 10-mile ride and three-mile run. Stumpie hurt, but that was to be expected.

The San Diego Triathlon Challenge was founded as a fundraiser for Jim MacLaren, the Yale defensive end turned super-BK triathlete. Jim's prominent triathlon friends stepped up and organized the race to purchase a wheelchair-accessible van after Jim's second accident. What the organizers had intended to be a one-time event went so well that they held it again the following year with hopes of making it an annual late season fun and philanthropic tradition.

The first year's financial goal was $25,000, but they raised $40,000. The second year's goal was $125,000 and they raised $140,000! (Today the Challenged Athletes Foundation, the offspring of the event, has a full-time staff and has raised nearly $3,000,000. The foundation has benefited hundreds of physically challenged athletes by providing funding, adaptive equipment and hope. The first Sunday in November remains one of my favorite days of the year. And Jim MacLaren is still my idol. To my knowledge, he's had more success in endurance sports than any other individual with a prosthetic leg.)

I was honored to meet Jim the day before the race that year at a media engagement in La Jolla Cove. I told him of my long-term goal to beat his marathon record time of three hours, 15 minutes. He offered moral support and commented that thanks to my smaller size, which is more appropriate for distance running, I could certainly do it.

One of the event founders, Bob Babbit—publisher of Southern California's *Competitor Magazine*, triathlon personality and all-around funky dude—was standing nearby when I made my statement. That night at the pre-race meeting, Bob introduced the disabled relay team of Allison, Shawn and me. He told the crowd of more than 100 athletes that my long-term goal was to break Jim's *Hawaiian Ironman* record! I stood in the back with a flushed face as the congregation turned and applauded. My mouth dropped. I didn't have the nerve to point out Bob's mistake (mistake?) and stood there half-smiling, enjoying the applause.

I had no intention whatsoever of attempting an Ironman, particularly the championships in Hawaii—arguably the toughest race of them all—but who was I to disappoint the crowd?

Our threesome completed another solid race the next day. Allison had another great swim, Shawn gave it all he had on the bike, and I ran the 13.1 miles in just under 1:43—eight-minute miles, better than I had hoped. The pain was there, but was not nearly as bad as in the beach run. The media coverage I received from that race, including the cover photo in the *La Jolla Light* and blurbs on both local NBC and CBS news shows, earned me another $1,000 from Balance Bar. Yahoo! Such a rewarding way to make ends meet.

I returned to Colorado to begin another year of ski racing with the Winter Park Team. I had several solid performances that year, but not enough of them. The weak link was my tendency to blow out of the race-course, nearly 50 percent of the time. It was important to me to make the U.S. team that season—1996/1997—in order to qualify for Japan in March of 1998. But my year-ending performance at Nationals at Mount Bachelor, Oregon gave the U.S. team coaches less than ample reason to consider me a worthwhile pick. The numbers simply did not justify an invitation.

The importance of their decision paled in comparison to the terrible loss my family experienced during the same week. My grandfather died the night before I left for Oregon. My father happened to be visiting me in Colorado when one of his sisters called with the bad news. Dad approached me just as I came into the room and, for an instant, two seconds maybe, he completely broke down in tears.

He regained his composure instantly. I had seen him on past occasions—usually one of my occasions—overcome with sadness, and this was another brief moment when I saw him lower his defenses, unable to hold back. His flash of vulnerability impressed me. It was somehow heart-warming to see him like this.

The next day, I flew as scheduled to the Bouldercsque city of Bend, Oregon, at the base of Mount Bachelor, where I met my good friend Kathy Holmes. She was touring the country clockwise from New York City and had just worked her way up the west coast. I told her about my Pépère's death and she offered to drive to me to the Portland airport that night, despite extreme whiteout snow conditions. It was a rare occasion when owning an SUV pays off. I caught the red-eye back to Boston.

Five other grandsons and I were pallbearers for Pépère's funeral. A fact I already knew was driven home at his services: everyone loved Pépère. Everyone who knew him held him, like Mémère, in high regard. The experience of putting him in the ground was tougher than I had expected after losing Rob. I thought dealing with a departed loved one would be easier the second time around. Wrong.

Pépère was one of 10 siblings to reach adulthood. Seven others died before they reached 10 years of age: one was stillborn, one died from appendicitis, and either Spanish Influenza or Sudden Infant Death Syndrome claimed the others. One of Pépère's sisters had 14 children, all reared in my hometown. Needless to say, his funeral was a big family reunion. The Martin clan celebrated my grandfather's life at the French Club on the afternoon of his burial.

I had flown back to Gardner to see Pépère the week before he died. The colon cancer he had battled for more than two years had spread to his liver and lungs. It was clear that his time was running out. In fact, he'd looked dead already. He was 30 pounds lighter than normal and had yellow skin and dark eyes. But he'd seemed to be at peace. He'd given me a watch my father had given him some years before. Then he'd told me a story.

Pépère was raised in a small town just across the border from the northernmost tip of Maine, home to my ancestors for 300 years. Back in the 1930s, during the Depression, Pépère's small town of Sainte Basille, New Brunswick, was poor and hungry like most of North America at the time. Facing a possible one-year prison sentence had they been caught, he and a friend, Edmund Cyr, headed out one day to hunt for food. The 15-mile hike to good hunting grounds took the better part of their first day in the forest. Pépère and his friend came across their chance to feed their families on the second day.

A female moose, six feet at the shoulder, approached the hunters' tree cover. Armed merely with one hatchet, the two made their way to either side of the huge animal with a strong intent to eat. (Intent—a very strong word.) Approaching her from opposite sides, the two got close enough to confuse the animal. Pépère took a swat and connected with her hind leg. She went down on a knee and Pépère tossed the weapon to his friend who then struck her opposing foreleg. While she lay on her side kicking wildly with what ability she retained, the brothers took turns passing the axe. They then butchered the moose, killed two deer in similar fashion, and dragged them all to a safe area on a sled they had manufactured out of pine branch and buried them in the snow. They spent the third day hiking back to town to secure a dog, a sled and more manpower. The two men were joined by Pépère's brother Hector and Edmund Cyr's brother Leo. The newcomers each suffered frostbite in their feet and were forced to make camp for the night. Pépère and Edmund Cyr dragged the meat back themselves and returned to the village of Sainte Basille the next day—heroes.

My grandfather, with his sixth grade education, was a hero. I knew that long before he told me the story. When I phoned my father that night and began to tell him of Pépère's heroics, he interrupted: "You've never heard the moose story before? If I had a nickel for every time I heard that one!"

Cancer, the cause of Pépère's demise, also claimed several of his brothers. But it doesn't stop there. My father is also a cancer survivor. At 33 (my current age), Dad lost a testicle to the disease. And my mother is a breast cancer survivor. That's a lot of cancer in one family. Is it enough to scare me? No.

I'm convinced that the cancer I would have had was in my left foot. All the more reason to lose it. Plus, the health battles my parents conquered helped establish a twisted common denominator that few families can claim: Dad's missing a nut, Mom's missing a boob, and I'm missing a leg. Go figure.

There may be a slew of cancer in the gene pool, but there are also a number of amputations in the family motor vehicle mishap annals. Two of my cousins, one second and one third, raised and still living in my hometown, are leg amputees resulting from car accidents.

Another story surfaced the week Pépère died: he had hidden his true identity from his children and his friends his entire life. His brother Arsene had died not long before Pépère moved to Massachusetts. Unlike my grandfather, his brother had a green card. Pépère took his brother's paperwork, used it to immigrate to the United States, and lived his life under that identity—celebrating false birthdays and everything. He somehow managed to keep it a secret his entire life. Bravo.

I believe a large part of my persistence in achieving whatever it is I set out to do has been passed down to me through generations of tough Acadien forefathers. Our Acadien heritage dates back to the early 17th century, when peasant farmers were forced to leave their land in southwestern France. They found solace in what is now northern Maine, New Brunswick, Nova Scotia and Newfoundland. Nearly 20 percent of the villagers died each winter in the early days. The British later exiled them from their new land to various areas—England, France and the American and French colonies. Many of these people eventually returned to Acadia and permanently established themselves.

The Cajuns of Louisiana come from the same blood lines. In 1636, my forefather, another Robert Martin, and his brother Pièrre arrived in what is now New Brunswick. Before long, Pièrre headed to Louisiana and helped secure the French presence that remains there today. The term "Cajun" comes from "Acadien"—try saying "Acadien" in your best Français. You'll hear the resemblance.

A small percentage of my lineage is also North American Indian. The Acadiens were friendly with the Mi'kmaqs (Micmacs) of the Algonquin family, and intermarriage was common. At some point in the 1800s, I believe, a forefather of mine married a Mi'kmaq woman.

In 1997 I traveled to St. Basille for a family reunion open to all the descendants of the 1636 Robert Martin. There are reportedly some 2,200 of us alive today of the 7,000 whose genealogy could be traced back to that man. Only 250 descendants attended. Of these, I was closely related to no more than 20. Many were seven or eight generations removed. I learned that day that I am the 12th generation to stem from a man kicked out of his homeland. We even have a family crest bearing French and Canadian symbols in quadrants of a Christian Cross. Pretty cool stuff. There's my genealogy, in short.

I returned to Oregon immediately following Pépère's burial. I had missed the downhill, my strongest discipline, which ran the day of the funeral, but I did compete in the remaining three races. I placed fourth in the super-G, crashed but finished the GS, and, embarrassingly, missed my start in the second run of the slalom. It was cold and raining and I stayed inside the lodge a bit too long. Oops.

With a lackluster ski season behind me, I left for an extended road trip.

Credit: Spofford Studio

Above: My family in 1990. That's Paty on the left and Elaine on the right.

Below: Albina and Ronald Martin—a.k.a. Memérè and Pepérè.

Credit: Wironen Studio

Above: Brent Ireland and me in the Rx7 before it was introduced to the fire truck.
Below: The Rx7 after it met the fire truck.

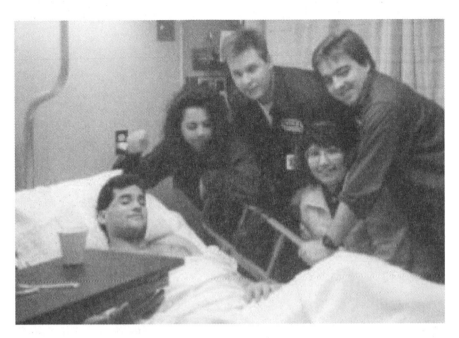

Above: Lincoln Electric training buddies visiting the hospital. Left to right: Katie (Jereza) Balko, Matt Atwood, Mary Lou (Gonzales) Rodriguez and Brendan McLellan.

Below: Paty and me taking a break at Mile 24 of the 1995 New York City Marathon.

Credit: Kathy Holmes-Robb

Above: Al Kovach and me climbing Hoosier Pass in the Colorado Rockies during the 1998 Tri4Life.

Left : First cycling gold medal at the 1998 U.S. Disabled Cycling National Championships in Tallahassee, Florida.

Opposite: 1998 Hawaiian Ironman Awards Ceremony…with a hurtin' Stumpie.

Credit: Mike Gladu

Credit: Das Foto

Credit: Das Foto

Opposite Top: Coach Ryan Crissey barking out my lap times in Sydney.

Opposite Bottom: Climbing Solerer Berg Hill of the 2001 Ironman Europe, in Germany, mile 90ish.

Above: The finish line of the 2001 Ironman Europe.

Above: Celebrating 2001 Hawaiian Ironman finish line.

Opposite Top: Skating against Team Russia for the 2001 U.S. Amputee Hockey Team in Washington D.C.

Opposite Bottom: Memphis in May Triathlon, 2001.

Credit: Action Sports International

One Man's Leg

Above: The hardware.

Dream Chasing

At some point during my younger years, around freshman year of high school, I had considered an acting or modeling career. Due to a fear of rejection, however, and probable peer pressure, I never acted upon that desire. The marathon experience removed any performance-based fears I had and provided me with all the confidence necessary to move in that direction. Commercial acting and/or modeling work, lucrative undertakings offering flexible schedules, could effectively finance my athletic ambitions if, by chance, I had talent in front of the camera.

While visiting Denver one day during the summer of 1996, I opened the yellow pages and boldly called the first talent agency that grabbed my eye—MacFarland Entertainment. My first meeting there offered both encouragement and opportunity; the staff appeared genuinely interested in working with me. Some talent agencies are notorious for building up hope, taking your money and producing nothing, so I kept my enthusiasm in check. The woman I met with told me, frankly, that I was too short for a modeling career but that my look might fit commercial print and film. I eagerly signed up for MacFarland's beginner acting class.

The first experiences in front of the camera were nerve-racking. Fortunately, as is the case when I face most new challenges, my anxiety subsided quickly. I sincerely enjoyed those Thursday night classes.

Performing among other neophytes helped ease my self-consciousness. The personalities in class were diverse: the young college girl, the high school kid with big dreams (who later would be represented in Los Angeles with a new stage name), the ex-military guy, a grandmother and a few others. Everyone in the group was committed at a different level, but we all wanted to give this acting thing a try.

Upon completion of the 10-week course, I had some photographs taken for promotional purposes. I chose a studio in downtown Denver;

the session included both head and full body shots.

It was October and, armed with my new photos, I left on my now-annual San Diego triathlon tour. I brought the shots with me, hoping to make some professional connections in the Los Angeles area. When I arrived, a friend in the prosthetic industry mentioned that a fax had come across her desk the day before from a New York agency looking for disabled models. Well, what do you know? I just happened to have my photos with me. I overnighted them to New York, and two days later, Curtis Gunn, the founder and president of the SHOT, wanted to sign me up.

I flew to New York a few weeks later to join a few other first-timers and several seasoned models to photograph for the inaugural SHOT profile book. I was in the company of Chris Waddell, a paraplegic member of the U.S. Disabled Ski Team and Paralympic wheelchair track racer; Heather Whitestone—Miss America 1995, who is hearing impaired; and Brian Frasure, one of the world's fastest BK sprinters. Allison Pittman, my tri-teammate, was photographed later in the week. A beautiful shot of her soon graced the cover of the SHOT Model Management portfolio.

In April, along with Allison Pitman and Chris Waddell, I returned to New York City to help promote the agency with an interview and photos in the *New York Times* fashion section. The spread was picked up by several papers across the country, and friends of mine in L.A. and Portland called to tell me they had seen me in some sort of modeling thing in their local newspapers. Some of them were impressed. Some of them laughed.

Curtis asked that I spend some time in New York City to further promote the SHOT. I was to meet with some of the players in the industry, create interest in the company and get us some work.

Brent Ireland, my good friend and roommate from my Lincoln Electric days in Cleveland, had relocated to North Jersey to handle the territory and customers that I had managed two years before. He let me stay at his place for the month, and because he was new to the area and had yet to develop many friendships, the camaraderie worked well for us both.

One evening Brent said something that I think about every so often when I find myself trying to fit in. He said, "I'm through trying to be what other people want me to be. They'll just have to like me as I am."

I've always liked him the way he is, and I have a great deal of respect for him and anyone else bold enough to simply be who they are.

While in New York City, Erik, the prosthetist at the Joyce Center, built me two new prostheses, one ski leg and one run leg.

I received the new run prosthesis a few weeks before the 1997 Amputee Track & Field Nationals in Springfield, Massachusetts. The new Flex-Foot was not much different from the everyday leg that, until then, I had also worn to run. It was the same model but with a stiffer ankle at a greater degree of plantarflexion (greater angulation at the ankle). It more closely matched proper form while running. It also had a longer working foot—and did not require a mechanically useless foot cosmesis, allowing for an extra three-quarters of an inch of carbon fiber to provide more leverage and power.

In Springfield, I competed both on the track and in the pool. I entered the 100-meter freestyle swim knowing from the moment I signed up that I would not stand a chance against the nation's best swimmers. There were a number of BKs there who could, and did, humble me.

The track, on the other hand, treated me very well. In the 1500-meter event, I ran against Gilberto Alavez of Mexico and Mark Soldo—a fellow patient of the Joyce Center—as well as a few others. These two came in second and third, respectively, in the same event at the MIT games in '95.

I was somewhat cocky, but my game plan in Springfield was to go out hard, wear everyone down and win without any fuss. I also had a strong intention to come in under five minutes. My best time in training was a 5:09, so I figured since I was already 11 seconds ahead of my own national record, I could count on a win at the very least. I was wrong. Again.

Mark took the field out strong but soon fell back. I then took the lead and worked a simple strategy: I ran as fast as I could. I led through 1350 meters with Gilberto in my back pocket. I could hear and feel him breathing throughout the entire race. He passed me on turn three and picked it up around turn four. I gave it all I had until he crossed the finish line less than 10 meters ahead of me. Conceding to a second place finish, I let up the pace with a few feet to go. As I approached the line, I glanced at the clock, which read 4:59.90. Bummer. The next couple of strides took exactly 0.7 seconds and I finished in 5:00:60. It was short of the goal, but respectable, nonetheless. Gilberto ran a highly impressive 4:58.90. He was nearly 40 years old at the time.

My time would stand as the American record for two years (Gilberto's faster time would establish a new Mexican national record), until Joe Lemar, also from Massachusetts, would break it in 1999 with a time of 4:51:97. Impressive. (But not as impressive as 15-year-old Andrew Lester's record-shattering time of 4:39 and change, posted in 2001!)

I have to admit, I was actually shocked that I did not win with the time I posted. I walked away saying aloud over and over again, "I can't believe I lost!" I regret having beaten up an oak tree in disgust.

That night the local news station broadcast my disbelief. I must say, I looked a bit silly. Ironically, in the process I earned a couple of thousand dollars from Balance Bar for both TV and newspaper coverage. Gardner was just 50 miles away and the media wanted to cover a local competitor. Lucky me.

My original plan had been to head back to Colorado after Nationals, but this didn't work out. The SHOT had yet to gain any significant momentum, but Curtis and I both wanted the company to prosper, so we came up with a compromise: if I would stick around, he would cover reasonable rent in the city.

It took a few weeks, staying with Brent in the interim, but I found a place for $400 a month in Stuyvesant Town at First Avenue and 16th Street. It was a room in a friend of a friend's apartment—and the place was a dive. My roommates were smokers and the place had a funk beyond the working limits of Lysol. The furnishings in my room consisted of a folding chair, some sort of pad that constituted a bed and a few borrowed blankets. I didn't enjoy living there, but for a couple of months in Manhattan at no cost to me, I could put up with it.

In the end, Curtis did not have the connections, expertise or savvy to launch a modeling agency despite having taken a legitimate stab at it. The only worthy occurrences during that entire summer were a publicity piece on the E! Channel and an interview with *SHOOT* magazine, the commercial film advertising industry's trade publication. Curtis did finance my temporary residence for 10 weeks in a safe area of town. Kudos to him for that.

Just days after my arrival in New York, I met an inquisitive woman in Central Park who was intently watching my friend John Siciliano, an AK Paralympic sprinter, work on his starts.

Suzanna Dalton introduced herself to us and mentioned that she was an actress and also taught the craft in her home two nights a week. John is an accomplished actor himself and, since I had taken some classes also, the three of us enjoyed an interesting conversation. Suzie was a regular on "All My Children" in the '80s—Nurse Somebody—and had appeared in guest spots on several sitcoms and series around that time. When she wanted more time to raise her son, who was in high school at the time, Suzie pursued commercial screen and voiceover work. Her most popular role was that of the Dulcolax Lady. She was the face of that popular laxative for several years. You might remember her curly strawberry blonde hair. Before our chat came to a close, I had talked my way into free acting classes. And a new friendship had begun.

Suzie thought that I should get involved in an acting internship to gain a little credibility. She recommended the Ensemble Studio Theater at 11th and West 52nd, near Hell's Kitchen, as a great place to investigate. A young friend of hers was currently interning there, meeting key people, getting some valuable training and adding an "Internship" bullet to her résumé.

I met with the theater's administrators later that week, and before my next class with Suzie, I was an intern at EST.

Things were falling into place a bit faster than even I was accustomed to. My path seemed to be paving itself in front of me as I walked. It was as if there was something out there looking after me, and this provided an almost unwavering confidence in what might lie ahead.

Dr. Wayne Dyer might describe me as a reverse paranoid. He wrote, in *Your Sacred Self*, "I sometimes think of myself as a sort of reverse paranoid. People who are paranoid believe that the world and everyone in it is out to harm them in some way. I think of reverse paranoids as people who believe that the world and everyone in it is out to provide for them, to protect them and to do them some good."

I believe that Suzie and I were introduced, by the Indefinable, to do me some good. When she and her son took respite at the Jersey shore for the summer, one of her students recommended another coach, Dr. Marianna Lead.

Marianna taught a class incorporating self-hypnosis, the field in which she had earned her PhD. I audited her workshop one evening and immediately signed up to study with her. Self-hypnosis proved to be an interesting twist that lent itself nicely to getting into character, as well as to athletics and overall peacefulness. I regularly use her "breathe in blue, breathe out red" technique to help relax myself on race day. This helps me focus my energies on the matter at hand: going fast.

I practiced and performed my first monologue in one of Marianna's classes. The piece was from a contemporary play in which the character is both love-struck and self-loathing, causing him great despair and anxiety when his girlfriend leaves him. My nerves were firing when I got up to perform the piece in front of the others for the first time, and the emotional state I was in played perfectly into the character. Upon completion of my debut monologue, Marianna said, "Amazing…You certainly have what it takes."

Under Marianna's tutelage, it is mandatory for all students to comment on their fellow classmates' performances. The five or six other students in my class had nothing but positive and encouraging words for me. One said I appeared to be "a seasoned performer." The overall feedback indicated that I had the necessary skills to pursue a career in acting. What a wonderful feeling it was to be told that I might have what it takes to fulfill a longtime secret ambition.

I began auditioning in the city while I was still taking classes with Marianna. Casting information for smaller films, commercial work, voiceovers and stage work was typically found in *Backstage*, a film industry publication in New York. Independent, non-union and SAG (Screen Actors Guild) film auditions were regularly pursued by every non-established, struggling actor in the Big Apple. Casting directors typically request a headshot and résumé for consideration for a particular part in a production. The hopeful submits a request to audition for one or more of several parts described in the casting call. Occasionally, landing an audition requires a telephone call during a specific and typically tight time slot. I landed my first audition that way in a small but popular SoHo theater.

It was a Saturday trial for a part in a very low budget independent (indie) film called *Dating*, and it came after a fun-filled night in Manhattan with the Jack-and-Kathy crowd. Before my 11 a.m. slot, a bunch of us went out for brunch and enjoyed the traditional hair-of-the-dog Bloody Mary. I limited myself to just one. I thought it might take the edge off without impeding my speech too much.

I arrived at the studio uncharacteristically early to provide ample time to review the copy—industry jargon for what is to be read that day. Still nervous, despite the morning cordial, I sped through my first reading without much personality. After some direction, I read a second time. It went slightly better than the first but garnered the same reaction from Duke—the writer, director, producer and star—and his assistant. Duke said, "Good job." The assistant said nothing and did nothing.

Clearly, I not only needed acting experience but also auditioning experience. Yet, two days later I got a message informing me that I had won the part of Tom, the jerky soon-to-be-ex-boyfriend in the production. I assumed that Tom was one of the major players in the storyline and I was nothing short of stunned to discover that they wanted *me*.

When I met with Duke a second time I discovered that Tom had a mere two lines. Two improv'd lines. One line became, "That guy's got a date? What a boob!"

To my credit, Duke also informed me that 1,200 people had auditioned and 1,800 more had sent in headshots and résumés to land one of the 15 available parts. This, needless to say, was enough to satisfy me. Still, it was the only speaking part I landed all summer—and, sadly, I never saw the movie.

I submitted my headshot and résumé for six or seven parts a week and was usually called to audition for at least one of them.

One submission was for a superhero comedy production. I stated that I could be the first Detachable Man. I thought it was a pretty slick idea and apparently so did the producer. I received a callback to audition a few days later…on a Saturday when I would be out of town racing at the Triathlon National Championships. Another big break went out the window.

I went on one or two auditions a week for the remainder of that experimental summer—and got an additional zero callbacks. Producers threw me a couple of bones by inviting me to the set for several non-paying "extra" parts in various indie productions and local business commercials.

One of these extra calls was for a film called *Casanova Falling*. Amy Redford, Robert's daughter, starred in the film along with an actor who had recently starred in another romantic comedy opposite Penelope Cruz. My leg was hurting that day, so I tried to inconspicuously remove it a number of times on the set. Still, the fact that I wore a prosthetic became obvious.

I was talking with the casting director (CD) when I caught sight of a young woman waiting patiently for us to finish our conversation. When the CD parted, Amy Redford approached to introduce herself and inquire about my leg. What had happened? Was it a problem? She also asked what I was hoping to accomplish as an actor. I told her that I was a novice spending the summer in New York City testing the waters, and that I was committed to being an athlete for the time being. Like most strangers who strike up this typical conversation with me, she said, "That's great!"

Coming from the average passerby, this type of support is always appreciated and never taken for granted; coming from Amy Redford, it was particularly special. She told me about her new interest in acting and that she had been studying in France for the past year. This, she mentioned, was her first big role and she was a bit nervous about the whole thing.

Another notable extra call was for the indie film *Remembering Sex*. After a few days of playing phone tag with the CD, she finally instructed me to show up a day or two later on the set in Alphabet City. (A section of town between First Avenue and the East River near the Lower East Side named for its streets: Avenues A, B, C and D.)

The day before my scheduled shoot, I headed out for a run on one of my preferred routes: Stuyvesant Town west to the East River, clockwise around the southern tip of Manhattan Island, through Battery Park, north past the World Trade Center, east through Greenwich Village and SoHo and back to Stuy Town. As I neared the East River, I noticed a film in production near the ball fields and stopped to inquire. A grip, or "gopher," told me the production was indeed *Remembering Sex*. He pointed out the CD and I boldly introduced myself. The approachable young lady recognized me from my headshot. We talked for a bit before I thanked her for her time, told her I would see her the next day and headed back out on my run.

The next day on the set, things got behind schedule or the script changed, and the other three extras and I were told that, unfortunately, we would not be used that day. The CD apologized and informed us that she would make it up to us by inviting us back another day. The invite came the following week, and I was asked to be at the V.A. Hospital in the Bronx for filming.

I was used in two scenes that day. The first was in the center courtyard, which doubled as a college campus for the day's production. Playing a college student, I got myself noticed by getting up off a bench two or three minutes into the scene and accidentally dropping all of my books. The cast and crew got a good laugh at my expense. Take Two.

By then I had developed a good rapport with the CD and she invited me back for another day's shoot. Actually, it was a nighttime shoot on location at a restaurant near Union Square. Because it was an operating establishment, the director was only granted time to film from midnight to 10 a.m.

At the time, the Stanley Cup playoffs were underway and nearing the finals, so I met my marathon teammate, Jack Barr, at a midtown bar to catch some of the NHL action before reporting to the set. On the way out, I saw a small crowd gathering around a car I thought was mine, a blue Honda Prelude. I got a bit freaked when I saw the smashed passenger window, but I immediately recognized my car right behind the one in question. The relief was temporary. *My* passenger window was also shattered all over the sidewalk and seat. I didn't notice until later that a small bag with some clothes, a Sony Walkman and my daytimer were missing. I realized it after arriving at the set a few minutes late. There was little I could do besides complain, so I chalked it up to Life in the Big City and went about my business.

The job of an extra is not terribly exciting. As in alpine ski racing, there's plenty of "hurry up and wait." Once things got rolling, however, I was glad I had made the commitment. I received considerable on-camera time as a bar patron complete with close-ups and voiceless chatter with one of the principals. (No, I never saw that movie either.)

I called for my messages before returning home that morning; there was one. The woman whose car was burglarized in front of mine had walked around the block looking for some of her stolen items and had found the bag holding my clothes and daytimer. Only the Walkman had walked.

Triathlon training that summer proved to be a major physical challenge—Manhattan cannot be described as an ideal location for an endurance athlete. Central Park, thankfully, is the saving grace. The six-mile loop around the park is a great run, as is the 1.2-mile loop around the reservoir in the middle. The Reservoir Trail boasts the greatest number of runners of any trail in the world, understandably. It is a dirt path that lies in the center of a huge park in the middle of an otherwise concrete and asphalt island that some 1.5 million people call home, many of them runners. And the outside six-mile loop is the only place for reasonable bike workouts on all of Manhattan.

Residing on the island created a training challenge, but I was in an ideal central location from which to travel to races. On any given weekend, there was a race within a few hours' drive. I took full advantage of this and made trips to Cape Cod for the Hyannis Sprint Triathlon, Vermont for the Fairlee Great Triathlon, New Hampshire for the New England Triathlon Festival, Pennsylvania for the Wilkes-Barre Triathlon, Maryland for the National Championships and Long Island for the South Hampton Hospital Triathlon. I rewarded myself after each of these drive-to events with a pint of Ben & Jerry's ice cream on the ride home, typically, New York Super Fudge Chunk. In the modified words of Jim Morrison (which he borrowed from someone else), *I eat more ice cream any man evah seen.*

All but the Cape Cod race were Olympic distance (1.5k swim, 40k bike, and 10k run) or longer. I promoted my entry to these races through the local press and received Balance Bar media payments from most of them.

Early in the season, at the Cape Cod race, I was asked to spend some time with fifth graders at a Barnstable public school. Two teachers whom I had met in Hilton Head the previous April had invited me to speak to their classes if I was ever in the area.

Speaking to kids was something I was interested in, so I seized the opportunity when I found a race in nearby Centerville that would help justify the five-hour trip. My father's sister, Rachael, lived in nearby

Mashpee with her family and offered a place to stay.

The day before the race I spoke to fifth grade students in Barnstable about the opportunities presented to me after what might typically be considered a tragic occurrence, the loss of a limb. Determination and opportunity were the focal points of the discussion. The 10 year olds were enthralled by my pursuit of athletics when I had, in their minds, such a dramatic impairment. I brought several prosthetics to the talk: the run leg, the bike leg, the ski leg, the sprint leg and the hockey leg. These show-and-tell items were a big hit among the youngsters. Those little people had so many questions that I could not possibly answer them all before my allotted time expired.

I closed the discussion by telling the class, "Despite the tragedies that may happen in life, it's up to you to turn your lemons into lemonade."

While I was on my way down the hall to speak to another group, I felt a tug on my shirtsleeve. I looked down to see a young boy, who introduced himself as Johnny.

"Can I ask you a question, Mr. Martin?"

"Of course you can. Anything at all, Johnny."

"I'm blind in my left eye. How do I make that a good thing?"

Stunned for a moment, I tried to think of a suitable response. What came out surprised even me. "Well, Johnny, I race against visually impaired members of the United States Disabled Ski Team and the only reason they get to travel around the world representing their country is because they can't see as good as everyone else." He smiled and ran away.

Before I left, after my second presentation, one of the teachers approached me with a bright smile. "Thank you so much, Paul, for whatever you said to Johnny."

"Why? What happened?" I asked.

"He stood in front of his entire class just now, and for the first time he told them all that he was blind in one eye. He'd always been too shy to talk about it. Thank you so much."

Wow! I had just made a real difference in the life of a little boy!

I was hooked. Speaking to kids was undoubtedly something worth pursuing. Several weeks later I received beautiful letters and drawings from each of the children present that day. One drawing depicted three men on a podium: receiving a bronze medal was President Bill Clinton and on the middle tier stood Michael Jordan. I stood on top.

I stared at that drawing for the longest time. Then I cried for a while. How could a fifth grader place me above the president of the United States and MJ? I felt for a moment as if I was lying to these kids. Did I mislead them?

No, of course not. I told my story…and they liked it.

After the sprint race the next day, Rachael asked if I had any intention of competing in an Ironman event. I scoffed at the question, just as I had when Mike Joyce told me I'd be running a marathon someday. I told her that the New York City marathon took so much gumption and commitment—not to mention incredible tolerance for pain—that I couldn't fathom an undertaking like the Ironman. I simply had no interest in attempting it.

But I did extend my limits in the following weeks and raced in several Olympic distance events.

When that educational summer in Manhattan came to a close, I drove to Southern California to race in the San Diego Triathlon Challenge, where I chose to compete solo. Earlier in the season, I had considered going the half-Ironman distance if the Olympic distance races went well, which they had.

By that time, I had developed a number of friendships across the country. I had friends in Cleveland, Detroit, Chicago, St. Louis, Denver and Las Vegas. I stopped in each of these cities for a few days of fun and frolic. Because these friends had commitments to "real" jobs, I found time to either swim, bike or run at least a couple of days a week as I stabbed westward.

Two months after the big family reunion in New Brunswick, Dad and I separately drove the greatest distance the contiguous United States has to offer; from the tip of Maine to San Diego. I drove there to race; he drove there for the sake of touring the country with Lillian in an RV. They easily coordinated their adventures to accommodate a rendezvous to spend some time with me and watch the race in sunny southern California.

That year's race was definitely a challenge. The 1.2-mile swim delivered a dose of humility. Willie Stewart, an above-elbow amputee and member of the U.S. Disabled Cross Country Ski Team, and I were the only two challenged athletes competing solo. The local newspaper chose to do a story about the two of us going to battle. The article quoted me saying, "I'll take him in the water, on the bike we'll be pretty even, and he'll destroy me on the run." Then it read, "One-Arm Willie not only beat Paul on run and the bike, but he beat him in the swim, too!"

Yep, a one-armed man beat me in the swim—in his first triathlon! At dinner after the race, Willie told me that his motivation was not to be beaten by "Model Boy." My run time of two hours plus was short of the 1:45 split I had hoped for, but my overall time of just over six hours provided ample satisfaction.

I learned that year that the International Triathlon Union (ITU) had a division for physically challenged triathletes at its World Championship event. (The ITU is the international governing body for the sport of triathlon. As a result of the work of this organization, triathlon would make its debut as an Olympic Sport at the 2000 Summer Games in Sydney, Australia.)

Let me make something clear. The sport of triathlon is most widely associated with the Hawaiian Ironman, a race born in 1978 when three beer drinkers argued which was more demanding: the 2.4-mile Waikiki open water swim, the 115-mile cycling race around Oahu or the Honolulu Marathon. They decided to merge the three of them (in doing so they cut off three miles of the bike portion to coincide with the start of the marathon), staged a race and 15 men embarked on a legendary day to earn the right to each be called an Ironman. A beautiful story, really.

The race was made famous by the ABC broadcast in 1982 when Julie

Moss, looking like she would be the new woman's champion in her first attempt at this distance, collapsed just feet from the finish line and, while struggling several times to get to her feet, was passed by Kathleen McCartney. The viewers were awed by this seemingly fragile woman's determination to get up and wobble her way to the finish line for second place.

The World Triathlon Corporation (WTC), which as of this writing stages 17 Ironman events around the world each year, is a separate entity from the ITU. Sprint distance races vary in length but are always shorter than Olympic distance. Long distance races vary and fall somewhere between Olympic and Ironman distance. A half-Ironman is considered a long distance event.

The 1997 ITU Triathlon World Championships were being held in Perth, Australia in November. A year earlier, thanks to the undying work of one of our own, Clarinda Brueck, a congenital arm amputee and die-hard triathlete, the ITU had recognized the Physically Challenged (PC) division. The qualifying criterion for all PC athletes was a sub four-hour Olympic distance race. I had already posted a fast enough time earlier in the summer, so when I learned of the opportunity to compete for Team USA, I had already qualified. I immediately got on the horn to petition financial sponsors to help me pursue a world championship. Balance Bar, Össur (my bike leg manufacturer) and Brooks Sports chipped in to make the trip possible. En route to Australia, I rendezvoused in Los Angeles with a BK amputee friend I had competed against in several track events, Mark Soldo. He had also earned the chance to compete overseas. In September, he had competed in his first triathlon and qualified to compete in the World Championship event.

I think Mark must have been a little nervous on race day—he had an epileptic seizure less than 10 minutes before our 6 a.m. start. When I saw him just a few feet away lying on his back, shaking violently, I thought at first that he had slipped and fallen and was making a joke of it, because he hadn't told me of his condition and he's such a practical joker. When I realized he wasn't fooling around, I called—OK, I screamed—for a medic. Since the biggest race of my fledgling career was about to begin, I could only wish him well and head to the water. I later learned that Mark came around and was fine by 6:20 a.m., but for good reason the officials would not let him race.

I was still not much of a swimmer and was bested by several other BKs in the water. The leader, Brazilian Paralympic swimmer and cyclist Rivaldo Martins, came out of the water in 22 minutes, while it took me a full 33. It didn't take me long to catch two other athletes on the bike, but I didn't even glimpse Rivaldo again until the run. Mark informed me in the bike/run transition area that I was still about 10 minutes behind Rivaldo. I ran hard and at the 5k point I saw him ahead of me, doing the same.

I felt my chance at victory sour. My run split was a couple of minutes faster than his and my bike split a couple of minutes slower. All said and done, the swim was my demise; he won by 11 minutes overall—the same amount of time I lost in the water.

Rivaldo beat himself, though, by making one huge mistake. He failed to submit the proper paper work and led the race director to believe that he had. Therefore, he wasn't officially qualified to compete. Not being one to take such deceit lightly, Clarinda stripped him of his championship status and awarded it to me. (Actually, it was sent to another Paul Martin triathlete in Colorado, and I didn't get it until eight months later when I just happened to meet Paul in the pool one morning.)

What can I say? I was not particularly proud of that avenue to world champion status, but I accepted it just the same.

Rivaldo and I both know who really won.

Badasses:
The Transcontinental Triathlon
for Life

Before I left to race in Australia, I spent a few days in Los Angeles with my friend John Siciliano, the Paralympic sprinter and aspiring actor. He had recently moved into the Hollywood hills to commit to a thespian career. Lenny Kravitz, the fashionable rock star, lived across the street. John was new to the neighborhood and hadn't actually *seen* Lenny yet, but he let me know nonetheless. (John has since written and starred in his own successful off-Broadway production, *Siciliano*, chronicling his own life on one leg. He has performed the play, along with a small cast, in Los Angeles and New York. By the way, when I was 14 years old, I figured out why they say "break a leg" in this business; so you can be in the "cast.")

John was enrolled in USC's graduate theater program with free tuition and room and board provided by the "Swim With Mike" scholarship program. This endowment was founded in honor of one of the university's All-American swimmers, Mike Nyeholt, after a 1981 motorcycle accident left him paralyzed. Like Jim MacLaren, Mike had some great friends who got together to stage a fund-raiser on his behalf. The affair now raises money for a foundation to benefit student athletes who have suffered a debilitation.

The inaugural event was dubbed "Swim For Mike" because he was not yet physically able to get in the water. He soon learned to swim again and has gotten wet at each and every gathering since. Hence, "Swim *With* Mike."

From Los Angeles I ventured to Santa Barbara to visit my friends at

Balance Bar, located just south of the picturesque southern California city, and to meet with a newly-found friend, Jim Howley. In 1997, Jim founded and completed, solo, the Transcontinental Triathlon for Life, a 3,300-mile swim-bike-run from Los Angeles to New York City, to raise awareness and funds for the battle against the AIDS virus.

Jim had been fighting AIDS since 1989, just a year after being diagnosed as HIV positive. He granted himself a "last wish"—to complete a sprint triathlon before the six months the doctors gave him to live ran out. He found that the training, even though it was against doctors' recommendations, made him feel better. The strength Jim gained not only made life more enjoyable but also helped his T-cell count—the benchmark for immune system measurement—begin to climb. The doctors were astonished by this person who hardly had the internal systems to defend against a common cold and yet found the strength to compete in such a demanding sport as triathlon. Over the next several years, Jim became competitive in triathlon and challenged himself further by conquering longer distance races. In 1996, he was awarded a slot in the prestigious Hawaiian Ironman Triathlon World Championship, the Tri-World Mecca, where he completed the 140.6-mile test in less than 15 hours.

NBC featured Jim as an outstanding competitor in their annual award-winning Ironman broadcast. He became a national spokesperson for the health benefits of exercise for AIDS patients, and soon founded A.I.D.S. (Athletics Instead of Depression and Sickness, later named Athletics, Inc.) and Positive Challenge, both non-profit organizations that benefit challenged individuals of all types.

I had read about Jim Howley and the Transcontinental Triathlon for Life in a men's health magazine. In the article, Jim invited disabled and non-disabled individuals alike to participate in the second annual "Tri4Life." Excited about the idea of pushing myself outside my current comfort zone while benefiting others, I tried to get involved, but somehow failed to get through the proper channels. Several weeks later, as it's prone to do, serendipity surfaced.

At the 1997 San Diego Triathlon Challenge pre-race meeting, I grabbed a back row seat next to my friend Al Kovach, the 1996 Superfrog Triathlon race director I had become acquainted with when Shawn, Allison and I teamed up the year before. A retired Navy SEAL, Al became an incomplete quadriplegic in a 1991 skydiving accident. (He retains the majority of the use of his arms, but that's not the technical definition of "incomplete." It has something to do with being able to feel your privates. Having sensation down there, that is.) After his accident, Al began training for a marathon and went on to win his division in the Los Angeles Marathon five years in a row. He also raced on the track at the Atlanta Paralympics. If you see him, ask him if he won a medal. He didn't, but ask him anyway.

Al told me that he would be covering the run section for a relay team comprised of Eric Neitzel, a spina bifida-afflicted athlete who would be tackling the bike segment in a handcycle, and Jim Howley swimming.

"Really?!" I perked. "Where's Jim?"

"On your left."

It truly was amazing. The more I experienced life in general, the more I recognized the importance of following the path that comes most naturally to me. During my adventures I had taken many turns that had been neither clearly marked nor frequently traveled. Somewhere along each trail I met someone or experienced something that influenced my decisions at the next crossroad.

I was learning that being yourself is possibly the greatest success any person can achieve. To be anything less than who you are compromises the ultimate goal of happiness. The only worthwhile undertaking, while we are blessed with the opportunity to enjoy life, is to be happy. The only way to truly be happy, I believe, is to be at peace with yourself. You never actually find a time and place where happiness "exists," but if the path you're on makes you happy, you're going the right way.

The fortuitous meeting with Jim led to an invitation to participate in the 1998 Tri4Life. My idea of participation consisted of a two-week stint somewhere along the route. Jim's idea of participation was the entire 65-day journey. He managed to spark my interest, but I did not hastily commit to such a tremendous undertaking. I had yet to bike more than 60 miles in a single day! One hundred miles a day, five days a week for nine straight weeks, seemed a bit drastic.

That night I returned to John's place in Los Angeles, and he convinced me that any choice short of going coast to coast would be the wrong one. The résumé, the fitness level and incorporeal experience were all in favor. The trip was also fully sponsored, and I would probably save money in the end—no food or rent payments for two months.

I called Jim to commit first thing in the morning.

The decision to self-propel myself across the country wrapped up the summer's competition, and I headed back to Colorado for the start of the ski season. The Winter Paralympics were a scant five months away, and my goal to compete in Nagano, Japan was still within reach. Somehow, I would be invited. I was sure of it. There were four races left in which to qualify, or more accurately, four races left to impress the national team coaches: the Huntsman Cup in Park City, Utah; the Eastern Regionals in Waterville Valley, New Hampshire; the World Cup Finals in Breckenridge, Colorado, open to the host country's non-national team members with sufficient national ranking; and the Columbia Crest Cup, on my home course in Winter Park.

The early January race in Park City was a minor disaster. I crashed hard and suffered both a broken shoulder and a concussion. (The shoulder injury—a chipped greater tuberosity—still bothers me.) Fortunately, my fourth concussion was merely second degree. I regained my consciousness, after being out for nearly two minutes, with the Winter Park Team's endlessly dedicated team director and founder, Paul DiBello, on the verge of administering mouth-to-mouth resuscitation. To know Paul is to know you don't want him to have to do that to you. As I came to, his bearded mug was my immediate out-of-focus image. Nightmarish!

At first, I did not know why he and the others were gathered around me. I didn't even know that I was lying on a GS course or that I was in Park City, UT. I really didn't have a clue what was going on at all. As I became aware of my predicament, I realized that an anxious racer waited in the starting gate, impatient for the ski patrol to drag me off the mountain and clear the course. Waiting in the start gate is not an enjoyable situation for any ski racer.

Following rudimentary checks for neck and back injury, it became clear that I had suffered nothing more than shoulder damage. I remember little about the ambulance ride or the emergency room other than the words "fracture of the right arm" being muttered by the attending physician who glanced matter-of-factly at the x-ray.

"There goes Nagano," I said to the nurse. She returned a look that was both sympathetic and quizzical.

According to the doctors, the injury would take six to eight weeks to heal. The Eastern Regionals were out of the question. The Breckenridge World Cup Finals would be a stretch, but I had faith that five weeks later I would be able to compete there in those critical Paralympic roster-qualifying races.

I had several weeks to kill while waiting to recover from my injury. I spent time in the weight room and I ran a lot too. According to friends, that was pretty comical; a guy running down the road with a carbon spring for a left leg and his right arm in a sling. Hey, what else was I gonna do? Watch Jerry Springer?

Sufficiently healed to race by mid-February, I somehow beat the majority of the U.S. team in the downhill at the World Cup Finals (they had bad wax!), and a trip to Nagano finally seemed secure. I only needed to finish the remaining races in respectful times to justify the overseas investment. Supportive national team members bolstered my confidence, ensuring me that I would be joining them in Nagano. I finished the super-G the next day and the GS the day after that—both marginal performances. My already shaky slalom skills were compromised by my shoulder injury. I had a typical bad day on the short course, hooking a tip and blowing up on the second gate, approximately three seconds into the race.

I still felt confident that Herman, the U.S. team head coach, would pick me to be part of the team. Rumor had it there was enough cash to take three more contending athletes—one was sure to be me.

Wrong *again*.

I was not on the list when the Paralympic team was announced. Refusing to be defeated, I lobbied for myself by telling Herman that I deserved to be there and was confident that I would do well. His response was, "I think you're too confident, Paul. Any idiot can ski fast."

The ski season ended a few weeks later, and with the whole mess behind me I decided to focus on the upcoming triathlon season. After a couple of weeks of biking in the hills of the Fraser Valley, I headed to Los Angeles to begin my arduous trek across America with the Transcontinental Triathlon for Life.

The trip began on the world famous Santa Monica Pier at 9 a.m., April 19, 1998. You would think the moments preceding a bicycle ride across the entire continent would be somewhat nerve-racking. Truth be told, the anticipation of a unique experience commanded my attention. We were about to ride our bikes from Los Angeles to New York City! What *badasses!*

At some point before departure, an avid cyclist told me that the right way to start any eastward cross-continental ride is to dip your back wheel in the Pacific at departure and the front wheel in the Atlantic upon arrival. Needless to say, I dipped.

At my side on the starting line was Kathy Urshel, an athlete who'd lost her hearing and vision at the ages of 21 and 28 respectively. Each had begun to deteriorate in her teenage years and eventually progressed to total failure. Her condition had been documented in numerous case studies, but the cause of each loss remained a mystery. Kathy won a cycling silver medal at the Atlanta Games (and would also make the trip to Sydney with Team USA in 2000. Blind riders compete on tandem bikes and take the rear, or "stoker," position. Kathy raced in Australia despite suffering a major crash on the track that resulted in a stroke and partial paralysis to her left side). Kathy is a badass.

Al Kovach and Jim Howley were also there, along with 50 members of the Triathlon Zombies, a local triathlon club who rode the first 20 miles with us as a proper send-off.

The journey started out a bit rough. We got lost just trying to get out of the city limits. But we made it through the first day with only minor grumbling from both the athletes and crew members.

Things continued to be less than organized for the next several days. Feeling strong on Day Two, I rode out several miles in front of the group. As I approached an intersection, one of the support vehicles caught up to inform me that I was going the wrong way and they would have to take me back to a designated meeting area. Two hours later, after a brief meeting and an hour of riding, I found myself at the very same intersection! *The bugs will work themselves out,* I told myself. *It will get better.*

Later that day we found ourselves late for a media engagement with the mayor of Palm Springs, so we thought it best to SAG: Support And Gear. (SAGging is loading into the support vehicles and driving onward.) Our radios were out of range with the other support vehicles, and for some reason the cell phones weren't working either, so we were forced to leave a crew member on the side of the highway—with one bottle of water, in the desert's glaring sun—to wait for the remaining SAG vehicle and inform them of our rush to meet the mayor.

Again, I told myself it would get better. But by the time we got to Palm Springs, we were an hour late and the mayor had departed for another appointment. The media was there nonetheless and we received some good press in the popular retirement town.

We had a team meeting that night to discuss how we might avoid such problems in the future. This crew had never been responsible for a group of cross-country riders before and they were learning as they went. Their efforts were not unlike my own heuristic approach to most activities: learn as you go.

And it did get better.

As we rode across the Mohave Desert toward Las Vegas, the sun scorched us for five straight days; sunscreen only minimized the damage. I had a heart rate monitor tan line for the next nine months. (You should wear a shirt when riding across the desert...duh.) My semi-permanent tan line paled in comparison to Al's problems.

Al lost his ability to sweat when he was injured, as do many quadriplegics. The lines of communication were cut between his brain and whatever glands control what should be an automatic bodily function. He carried a little squirt bottle to cool himself off through the more tolerable stretches of road.

Somewhere in Nevada, cruising downhill at 35 m.p.h., Al's handcycle went into a speed swivel with a tractor trailer on his tail, and he crashed. He lost some skin and did some minor damage to his bike. But he kept riding: another badass.

As we rode toward Las Vegas, I learned to appreciate both the country Americans are blessed to call home and the power of the human spirit. Here were four individuals, each with a significant physical challenge, swimming, biking and running thousands of miles across America to show anyone who might take notice that, despite adversity, anything is possible. My challenge was by far the least disabling of the group's: my life is not threatened by any disease, my world is as accessible to me as it is to any able-bodied individual, and I did not rely on others to get around in strange places.

My new friends demonstrated the unique and often indomitable spirit of humanity. I have coined this domain of people's capacities thisAbility: the unyielding drive to achieve despite obstacles. To get past these hindrances we sometimes need help from others. So, I say, go ahead and ask for it.

One barrier I had to deal with was the improper fit of my cycling prosthetic. Prior to the Tri4Life, I had ridden few consecutive days of any appreciable distance. In the first two weeks of our ride, I suffered large and painful blisters behind my knee where the posterior trim line of my socket constantly worked against the skin. This problem provoked sympathy from the team but also provided a dose of dark entertainment, not unlike most of my misfortunes. The crew heard me howling in pain each morning at the onset of the day's ride as the first few pedal strokes would grind my open blisters, which eventually numbed. When I got on the bike, people stopped talking.

As the days passed, I modified my socket in hardware stores and machine shops along the way. I ground away material and built new socket trim lines with several types of moldable materials I purchased. By the time we reached St. Louis, six weeks into the trip, I had a good fit and my blisters had healed. I sent my modified socket to the Össur prosthetist in California so that he could make me a permanent socket of matching form. I rode with my walking leg until we reached Chicago a week later. Once there, the leg builder forwarded my newly duplicated permanent socket to our hotel.

America's natural beauty is uniquely showcased from the saddle of a bicycle. Beginning with our ride through the desert, we saw just how spectacular a barren landscape can be with a distant mirage and backdrop of faraway snow-capped mountains. In Moab, Utah we witnessed the awesome Double Arch in Arches National Park. Several of us lay silently underneath the magical rock bridges at sunset. For nearly 20 minutes, no one said a word.

We learned a lot of little things about our country along the way. For instance: tumbleweeds are hard to hit; Hannibal, Missouri is all about Mark Twain; broken glass exists continuously from coast to coast; and there's an astonishing amount of road kill out there. I was shocked to see five or six kills a day: possum, deer, snakes, raccoons and a monkey. Just kiddin', no dead monkeys, but Jim swore he rode by one. Fittingly, we even met a lady at a Pennsylvania campground with a three-legged dog and another dog in a little doggie wheelchair.

People wanted to help. All kinds of people wanted to do all kinds of things. One of the mechanics who had helped me with a bike leg modification gave us cash out of his pocket—and got his workers to kick in, too. Small town motels gave us free rooms most nights. KFC, Pizza Hut and Subway fed us dozens of meals free of charge. Both the St. Louis Cardinals and the Chicago Cubs gave us free tickets for games.

This was the summer of the McGuire/Sosa homerun rally. Of course, we got to our Cardinals game in the fourth inning and McGuire had hit one out of the park in the second. Sammy came up short the day we saw him swinging in Chicago.

Even the folks at a Cleveland movie theatre spotted us a complimentary show. It would be nice to think that everybody was so friendly, but the Indiana punks who threw stuff at us from their passing pickup destroyed that theory.

As expected, there was plenty of fun to be had. We played racquetball in St. Joe, Missouri, rode nearly every ride twice at Cedar Point Amusement Park in Sandusky, Ohio and played a nine-hole round of golf in Philly. The nights by the campfire in the middle of the Nevada desert, in the Colorado forest and in Midwestern campgrounds were priceless. Strong friendships form when you spend two months on the road with people. The ongoing joke was, "A quadriplegic, an amputee and a guy with AIDS walk into a bar..." That's it. That was the joke.

In Chicago, we swam in Lake Michigan. At the lake that day, we met a woman who had lost her leg below the knee in those very waters the previous October. She'd been run over by a big yellow tour boat while training for her first triathlon! The day we met Kati was her first day back in the water. (Kati and I would compete together at a 5k race in Chicago a year and a half later, in 1999.)

Swimming in Chicago was one of three wet days that made the Tri4Life a true triathlon. We swam in the 55-degree water of the Colorado River in Moab—wetsuits came in handy—and later in Cleveland, in Lake Erie. But the real challenge from the Windy City onward was what separates many competitive triathletes—the run portion.

Joining us in Chicago was Sarah Reinertsen, who held several above-knee amputee running world records, including one in the marathon. (She would later take a position doing television commentary for both the Sydney Paralympic Games and the New York City Marathon.)

We had already run a few 5k races in various cities along the way, nothing too difficult. Each of the remaining days of the trip, however, would include a run before and/or after the day's bike ride. Between Chicago and New York City, a typical day would include a five-mile run in the morning followed by a 50- or 60-mile ride.

In a Pennsylvania luncheonette, I met a 300-pound guy named Tony with long hair and a beard. He was having lunch; I was taking a leak. Tony told me about a motorcycle accident that had caused a great deal of damage to his wife's leg. She'd been on crutches ever since, rejecting the doctors' recommendations to amputate. When the two of them had seen Sarah and me running down a country road the day before, his wife began to cry. That night she told him that she just might go through with the amputation after all.

Of the 65 days we spent on the road that summer, one week in particular stood out from all the rest simply because of the physical effort required. It was a six-day stint through Pennsylvania. On Day 53 of the trip, we ran 10 miles, biked 25, then ran four. Day 54 consisted of a 10-mile run before a 37-mile ride. Day 55 was "just" a run—a 20-mile run! I think I actually ran about 17 of those miles.

On Day 56, I could only run three or four of the scheduled 10 miles and walked the remainder. Stumpie was blistered and sore all over and simply couldn't stand the pounding anymore. Of course, we then rode 27 miles. On Day 57, I opted to walk the 10-mile run section before biking another 37. On Day 58, I walked the 10-mile opener once again and then biked 33 miles. Then we took a day off.

Jim's major incentive in establishing the Tri4Life was to launch a grant program. The Athletic Spirit Awards would be given to worthy youngsters throughout the country. He created the program to help physically challenged youth reach their athletic goals. Individuals or groups would be given racing wheelchairs, handcycles, prosthetics, cash and more. Once the program was established, several companies donated product or money to match the type of assistance the recipients requested. One of our tasks during this trip was to present these awards to young men and women as we progressed along our route to New York City.

In Los Angeles, for example, we gave a young hearing-impaired gymnast money to train toward her Olympic—not Paralympic—goals. Kerri Strug, the Gold-medal-winning heroine of the 1996 U.S. Olympic Team, presented the award. In Moab, Utah, a young man with spina bifida received a handcycle. In Denver, a boy received the same type of computerized hearing implant that Kathy used to help her interact with others. In St. Louis, we presented the local junior wheelchair racing team with money to travel to the Junior Nationals in Seattle. In Chicago, we helped send a young girl born with AIDS to a summer camp for kids affected by the disease. In Cleveland, a group of children with various disabilities received bicycles and running shoes. In Pittsburgh, a girl received a new wheelchair; a boy in Philadelphia got one too. Finally, in New York City we presented a young girl with cerebral palsy with a grant to pursue her athletic endeavors in a wheelchair.

These experiences helped reinforce my commitment to my current chosen occupation: go hard and true in the direction of athletics and represent all people's abilities. It has been a poverty-stricken and friendship-reliant pursuit, but I strongly believe it is a part of the purpose I was given.

Some folks think I am taking advantage of my situation to do what I enjoy instead of working a real job. My response is this: you're absolutely right! What better way to spend your days than pursuing your passions while giving others hope and inspiration? In my case, opportunity knocked in an exceptionally unique way, and not one I would necessarily welcome again with open arms. But everyone can give something to others. What each of us possesses is not always easy to see, and some of us might have to actively search for it. In my case, my amputation was that opportunity.

The final day of the adventure included a run across Staten Island to the Manhattan Ferry, where we enjoyed a welcome half-mile walk to the finish line. Fittingly, our fearless leaders billed this run a six-miler, but it turned out to be more like 10. An additional four miles at that stage seemed endless.

Once off the ferry, we walked the final mile to the front lawn of City Hall where—among a small crowd of media, several sponsors and city officials—my Dad waited. He, Lillian, Aunt Rachael's family and my good friends Suzanna Dalton, Holly Lehr and Amy Sind greeted us at the closure of our magnificent escapade. While Mom could not make the trip, I'm sure she was there in spirit, as were the children whom we helped along the way. I believe that these people, along with the billions of others who populate the world, made a trip like this possible. It's a collective energy thing, something I am only beginning to understand. It is the true meaning of community.

Another Lesson Learned

After the trip, I spent several days back home in Massachusetts. A few of those restful days were gratefully spent with a woman named Andrea. We had met at my sister Paty's wedding several months earlier and spent a good chunk of the evening together. I then visited her for a week in Boston, and she followed that up with a visit to Colorado.

This time, we shared a wonderfully intense few days together back in Boston. It was so wonderful that I considered trying to make something out of this long-distance relationship. The feeling was mutual. I enjoyed the ease of her company, the frequent laughter we shared and her beautiful smile. Andrea held my attention and my respect. *What should I do?*

Before I left Boston, we discussed the idea of Andrea moving to Boulder, getting her own place and taking a stab at life in Colorado. Then she suggested, "Just move back home and get an engineering job."

It suddenly became obvious that we had different views of the world. Neither worldview was better than the other; but the gap was great. Andrea's desire for security and certainty about the future kept me from committing. My path was not paved with certainty, nor did I want it to be. It was a major conflict and I was not willing to compromise. I would not jeopardize myself or a partner by creating a path that would lead to resentment.

Past relationships had taught me patience. I had never been burned by committing when I shouldn't have, it's actually the opposite. I believe that being true to yourself is too important, and the pain endured after a broken relationship does subside. Sue, Jenny and Lisa all taught me this.

Sometimes I wonder what Andrea did with that baseball—the one that was hit over the Green Monster, then over the net, at Boston's famed Fenway Park. It sailed over our heads as Andrea, Paty and I walked along Lansdowne Street. Paty said, "Hey, there goes the ball!"

I chased it down like a madman, on crutches, on a particularly bad leg day. Some other guy got to it just before I did, because I couldn't bend over fast enough. The crutches were stuck in my armpits. But he gave it to me minutes later when his buddies at the hotdog stand tore him a new one for taking it from a guy on crutches.

I gave it to Andrea that night.

Becoming Competitive

From Boston, I flew to Lubbock, Texas to compete in the Buffalo Springs Lake Triathlon, a half-Ironman distance race. I chose this event for several reasons. First, it had a reputation as a well-run race. Second, I would need to complete a race of this distance or longer to solidify my Hawaiian Ironman slot—should I be lucky enough to receive an entry through the physically challenged lottery held two weeks after this event. (Yep, one year after adamantly denouncing any desire to go to the ultimate triathlon distance, I felt the pull.) And finally, the conditions in Lubbock were similar to Kona—hot and humid, but not as windy.

In the middle of the nowhere called Lubbock, Texas, despite little time spent in the water in recent months, I had a good race with a respectable swim and a strong bike split. That put me in a position to potentially break five hours—a time 90 percent of the competitors, able-bodied or not, would be proud to post. Unfortunately, the run did not go quite as well as the swim and bike. I needed to complete the 13.1-mile section in less than 1:45 to meet my sub-5 goal. The searing heat—108 degrees when I crossed the finish line—worked against me and everyone else out there. Moreover, a problem with my leg suspension kept me from running at peak capacity. The sleeve that generates my primary suspension ripped, causing a tremendous amount of pistoning and, hence, blistering. For the last few miles, I could run no more than a hundred feet before the pain forced me to stop and dangle my prosthetic in relief for 30 seconds or so before running another hundred feet and re-dangling. With a couple of hundred yards to go, I turned the corner to see one side of the street completely lined with spectators—there was no way I was going to allow myself to stop in front of them. That short stretch remains the most pain-intensive run I have ever experienced. But I made it. When I crossed the finish line, someone handed me an ice-cold beer. Ten seconds later, the can was empty.

Funny how beer tastes better on some days than on others.

I returned to Colorado to the new residence I had arranged in Boulder after the Tri4Life. When I arrived, I found a surprise in the mail: a certificate proclaiming my status as the United States Olympic Committee's Disabled Athlete of the Year…for 1997? I received it in June of 1998. Somehow, not only had the voting committee failed to forward the certificate, but I hadn't even caught wind of the honor. Furthermore, I was ignorant of the fact that six months earlier I was in contention with the likes of Tiger Woods and Marion Jones for America's Athlete of the Year. I wasn't picked for the overall distinction, but, needless to say, I was proud to have been bestowed with the honor I did receive.

Months later I found it interesting that I was awarded this honor for 1997 while that year paled in comparison with what I managed to accomplish in 1998.

I was excited to venture out of the little mountain town of Winter Park to take root in the city of Boulder. The Olympic Committee's certificate was a wonderful way to christen my arrival, but what was more exciting was my first day back in the pool for a swim workout. I was still a relative newcomer to triathlon and hadn't met too many of the sport's big names. I arrived at Scott Carpenter pool in Boulder, where I was told the majority of triathletes train, and the first face I saw in the water was that of Paula Newby-Fraser. (The name is a household one—if you've ever even thought about doing a multi-sport event. Paula has won the Hawaiian Ironman eight times, more that any other man or woman.) Then I saw Peter Reid. Mike Pigg. Cam Widoff. All huge names in the sport.

It turned out that most of these athletes were just in town that summer for a week-long camp. Still, I was happy with my new home.

Two weeks later I made my bike racing debut at the 1998 Disabled National Cycling Championships in Tallahassee, Florida. Getting there was a challenge in itself. I was flat broke and hadn't been able to secure a flight. In the frantic few days that I was home, I pursued every frequent flyer friend I knew in hopes of getting on a plane. It came down to two friends, Dan Critchet—a fraternity brother, and Kathy Celo—a staff member at Disabled Sports/USA. Each of them worked right up until the last minute to get me airborne. At the airport just 24 hours before the first race, I lay back on my bike case at 5:30 a.m. in front of a bank of pay phones. I impatiently waited for a call from either Kathy or Dan, who were struggling to get me on a United Airlines flight. The next one to Florida left at 7:10 a.m.

With a half-hour to spare, Kathy called with good news; she had set me up with someone's miles and I could go ahead and board a plane to Jacksonville. From there I would have to find my own way to Tallahassee, a two-hour plus car ride. By the time I would arrive in Jacksonville, the latest bus would already have departed.

I was not too worried. Get me to the state of Florida and I would take it from there.

I was standing in the check-in line when I saw a pony-tailed, crutch-reliant, one-legged man carrying a set of race wheels. He fit the description of a cyclist I'd heard about from Denver.

"Rex?" I shouted.

"You must be Paul," he said. "I heard there was a BK here somewhere looking for a flight."

It turned out Rex was heading to Atlanta, getting a car there and picking up another cyclist. I mentioned I was booked to fly to Jacksonville but did not yet know how I would get to Tallahassee. "Why don't you fly with me to Atlanta. I'm renting a Blazer and there should be plenty of room for you and your bike." I immediately requested a flight change to Atlanta and the fine folks at United Airlines were happy to accommodate. Problem solved.

Rex's story is a classic lesson straight out of the School of Hard Knocks. He had been an alcohol and drug abuser in the early '80s when he lost his leg in a drunk driving accident. Obviously it was a heavy blow, but when all was said and done, perhaps that blow saved his life. He has since turned to a healthier lifestyle through athletics. Rex has earned

Paralympic and World Championship titles cycling—using only his right leg, with no prosthetic. He now shares his story with young people in an effort to help them achieve a better future.

In Atlanta, we picked up Dory Selinger, who also has an interesting story. In 1994, a deranged woman left her house on a murder mission; she intentionally set out to take someone's life, no one in particular. She succeeded by driving her car into a pack of cyclists, killing one rider—later claiming that he was the devil—and injuring several others. Dory had to have his right leg amputated below the knee. With his dreams of racing professionally seriously fogged, Dory began his quest for Paralympic medals.

The national championship time trial was held the morning after we arrived in Tallahassee. There were only four competitors in my disability category racing for the title. Dory, being the current national champion, was scheduled to race last, an earned advantage. In a time trial, racers are typically sent out every 30 to 60 seconds and compete as individuals without the benefit of another cyclist's slipstream. The fastest from start to finish wins. As the final racer, Dory had the advantage on the out-and-back course of knowing how the competitors in front of him were faring.

Pedaling across America for so many miles had done me some good. In the morning's time trial, I put my head down and rode my ass off, simple as that. The course went out and back on a single, flat road. At the turn around, I was psyched to see that I had Dory by about 30 seconds. Not over yet. I pushed, pulled and buried myself to the finish line. From the starting line onward, I wanted that first place honor—the honor of being the fastest one-legged road cyclist in the United States of America. In one hour and two minutes, I was that guy.

Dory may have had the advantage, but I had the strength and finished nearly two minutes ahead of his second place time. That day I earned the honor of being presented with the coveted Stars 'n Stripes National Championship jersey. Many cyclists have competed for decades in pursuit of one.

The next day was the road race. This classic event is at the core of bike racing and is the race all "roadies" want to win. On the line that day were the same racers who had competed the day before, plus one, Gary Seghi. Gary, a chiropractor from Austin, Texas, home of America's favorite cyclist Lance Armstrong, had raced professionally some 20 years ago—before he was hit by a truck while riding. The accident resulted in severe damage to his left leg. He retained his flesh and blood, but the limb lost an inch in length and suffered limited flexion at both the knee and ankle. Gary raced with us in what is, non-technically speaking, the "single side disability using both legs" category.

In a road race, all competitors start together and the first one to cross the finish line wins. It sounds simple, but drafting, teamwork and strategy are all very important, particularly in a big event with many racers.

This event, however, did not have the necessary number of riders to create true road race dynamics. There were five cyclists in our class alongside those with arm disabilities (wingers) and those in Rex's class, for a total of about 16 cyclists. At the Nationals, the various classes start together in an effort to increase the pack size and energy of the race. Soon the stronger racers, generally wingers and BKs, break away from the others and a race is born.

It was a hot and muggy day, typical July in Florida. The course had a few decent hills, but nothing too trying. Things got underway slowly. Most of the riders knew one another from the small disabled cycling community and chit-chat prevailed early in the race.

At the first good hill, which was also the final climb leading up to the finish line on the four-lap course, one of the wingers turned up the heat and soon Gary and I were the only two BKs in the lead pack. We were concerned only with each other, but we worked with the wingers to get away from the remaining BKs, primarily Dory. Each category retains its own gold, silver and bronze medals, so the arm amps were not concerned with us either.

On the last lap, another one of the wingers rode out hard, and the remaining three or four in that division chased him. Gary and I were alone on the road and studied each other carefully for the final several miles of the 45-mile course.

The finish line lay about 200 meters from the crest of a 200-meter climb. Halfway up the climb, with Gary on me like a shadow—as he had been for the last few miles, he's the smart one—I got out of the saddle to kick in the glamorous finish line sprint. Gary reacted quickly, and in doing so developed an instant leg cramp. This threw his line off enough to tangle his handlebars with mine, which sent him to the ground while I managed to keep the rubber side down. My immediate rookie reaction was to stop and pick him up, but I quickly snapped out of it and took off toward the finish line before he had a chance to get himself back together.

This was not the glorifying finish I had envisioned as we had slowly churned those last several miles, but it was another national championship. For my debut in disabled bike racing, two jerseys couldn't have tasted sweeter.

Rex, Dory and I left after the race and drove back to Atlanta so Dory could catch an evening flight. (You gotta appreciate competing against the best, beating him, then dropping him off at the airport.) Rex and I stayed at my friend Dave Grevemberg's place just outside the city. (Dave would later become the Director of Sport for the International Paralympic Committee.)

We got there late, around midnight, but one business matter remained: I had to check my e-mail for one particular message before the day could end. It was July 15, 1998; the day Ironman drew its physically-challenged division lottery slots.

I immediately jumped on the computer. There was a memo from Diane Bertsch of the Hawaiian Ironman staff: "Congratulations…" I got very excited. "…on your win at Nationals." My heart stopped beating for a second. "You've also been chosen to compete in the Hawaiian Ironman's 20th anniversary race."

"YES!" I exclaimed, waking up Dave's girlfriend. I was so incredibly…happy, nervous, stunned. Talk about a big couple of days!

We had a beer to celebrate and talked about how fabulous the race would be, and how much this would do for my self-confidence and my career. It was nearly 3 a.m. before I attempted to catch a few winks, but it might as well have been an all-nighter. I didn't sleep a minute that night thinking about an October trip to Hawaii and the cycling strength I hadn't previously known I possessed. We left for the flight back to Denver at dawn.

Several days after the Tallahassee races, the U.S. Disabled Ski Team had its first dry land training camp at the University of Colorado in Boulder, just a mile from my new home. I had learned of my invitation to the national ski team during the Tri4Life. We had celebrated that night at Eddy McStiff's tavern in Moab, Utah.

The mid-July camp, my first responsibility as a team member, involved some challenges I had not yet faced and didn't necessarily approach with the right attitude. I became very aggravated when I kept failing to properly tiptoe through the zigzag tire course. My temper flared and I embarrassed myself with verbal frustration.

Stop. Breathe in blue, breathe out red. Start over.

The primary objective of dry land camp was to jump-start the team into physical fitness for the upcoming season. The workouts consisted of running, resistance training and plyometrics (dynamic exercises using body weight as resistance). During one of these plyometric workouts, I literally overcame hurdles I previously considered impossible. The exercise was one-legged hops over 25 12-inch hurdles spaced 18 inches apart. The hurdles presented no challenge to my right leg, but I had no intention of even trying the exercise on my prosthetic side. Herman insisted I make an attempt. "You won't know if you don't try," he said. He was right.

After several tries, and failures, at the first few hurdles, I managed to get in a groove and eventually made it to the end without missing a single hurdle or putting my right foot down. If I gained anything from that camp—I was already physically fit from triathlon training—it was the satisfaction of having accomplished that one simple task.

Two weeks after camp, my focus was back on triathlon. The 1998 ITU Physically Challenged Division World Championships were held in Toledo, Ohio. Switzerland hosted the able-bodied race that year but, unfortunately, the course was deemed unsafe for wheelchair athletes, so our entire division was relegated to the Ohio venue. Most of us were disappointed with this decision since the energy we experienced in Australia could not possibly be duplicated in Toledo, with all due respect to Jamie Farr. But we unanimously chose to compete for the sake of building momentum within our division.

As in the days prior to my departure to Florida the previous month, I scoured my contact list in an effort to find a friend with frequent flyer miles to donate: no luck. So, I drove two 12-hour days from Boulder to Toledo. Clarinda set me up with a home stay—a local family willing to house athletes from out of town. Triathlon is great like that. I joined a rookie winger from England and we stayed with an obliging Ohio couple and their son.

Toledo was not the glamorous layout I would have enjoyed in Europe, but it did offer a tremendous cash savings (can you save what you do not have?) and a very fast course.

My main competition that day was Joel Sampson, a BK from Honolulu rumored to be a strong athlete, Mabio Costas, a Brazilian living in Manhattan, and two Midwesterners who had a couple of decades on the rest of us. Rivaldo Martins, the Brazilian who beat me in Australia, did not make the trip.

The flat bike course lent itself nicely to helping me set a new Olympic distance personal record. I shattered my previous best of 2:28:58 with a time of 2:21:26. Joel outran me but could not make up the 10-plus minutes I had gained over him in the swim and bike sections. Mabio made the classic mistake of trying something new on race day; he experimented with a supplement designed to help prevent dehydration typically experienced during hard, sun-baked workouts. The experiment backfired and caused an inability to urinate, which resulted in heavy cramps and a botched race. I drove home the next day a legitimate World Champion.

The year had brought many accomplishments, but they were not without some painful experiences. Specifically, I learned some hard-earned lessons about how to ride a bicycle.

It started with a crash in Kansas during the Tri4Life. The tandem and I were riding along the straight and endless Highway 36. Kathy and her pilot of the week, Mike Hopper, rode in front of me, to the right. A truck was approaching several hundred feet behind us, and Mike and I looked backward to check out the vehicle, each turning toward the other in the process. I drifted toward his rear tire, caught it with my front tire, and subsequently introduced myself to the pavement. I lost some skin on my right shoulder, hip and ankle and learned not to drift when looking behind.

Another important lesson in Bike Riding 101 came during a criterium race in Denver. A "crit" is typically a 40- to 60-minute race on a course one-half mile to a mile in length. In the first lap of my first crit, I came upon the start/finish line just as the pack began to sprint. As I got out of the saddle to join them, my handlebars turned 90 degrees and I kissed the asphalt at 30 m.p.h. I slid 40 feet on my right elbow, removing flesh that took six weeks to heal. The neutral support staff, trained to deal with such circumstances, was on the spot to quickly replace my severely damaged front wheel. I got back in the race the next lap.

In a crit, a rider with a mechanical failure or crash is allotted one free lap, so I jumped back in when the pack came back around. I wondered as I got back in the groove what could have caused the crash. The only explanation I could think of was that maybe my prosthetic had hooked the bottom of my handlebar when I got into the aggressive sprint position. This hypothesis came to me as we completed the lap and the field sprinted again. I stood up to sprint and my prosthetic hooked the handlebars, rotated them 90 degrees, and sent me sprawling toward the road again. This time, aware of the condition of the right side of my body, I managed to take the punishment on the left. My helmet met the road, accompanied by a severe bell-ringing. I crawled to the side, lay in the grass, and counted myself out of the race. Two medical staffers came to my aid and asked that I report to their tent for further evaluation and wound care. When I arrived minutes later, I asked, "Are you the same two doctors I saw a moment ago?"

"You're not going anywhere for at least an hour," one responded.

I was fine an hour later. Lots of bandages, but no concussion. The next day I cut an inch off each end of my handlebars. I also sent an e-mail to my friends and supporters, which I titled *Bike Racing Can Be Dangerous*, detailing the episode.

Not long after, following another mishap, I sent this one:

Bike racing is not dangerous . . . I am dangerous!

I picked up on this Saturday as I picked myself, my broken helmet and my broken sunglasses off the pavement. The road's shoulder narrowed by about 12 inches without me really noticing until it was too late. At the local convenience store, where I went to grab some Neosporin and Advil, my Body sat me down to have a few words with me. At this point I'd made it to the toilet and got down on my knees. I became itchy all over, sweaty and cold, I couldn't feel my lips or my fingertips, and I had a God-awful taste in my mouth I'd never had before.

Body said, "You know something, I'm not one of those sponsored pieces of equipment you don't seem to have any respect for!"

"But..."

"Shut up or I'll make you puke."

Thankfully, I didn't. I lay on the concrete floor with a wet towel on my forehead.

"From now on, every time you abuse me I'm gonna retaliate. How do you like the no-feeling-in-your-lips deal? OK. I have your attention. I thought the leg thing would have smartened you up a bit but noooo. You gotta go and break me skiing and jump off bicycles at

high speeds. Well, enough is enough! Cut the crap or next time I'll make life a little more miserable. Good day!"

That being said I started to feel a whole lot better (t + 1.5 hours). Luckily, my new friend and riding partner, Sue Latshaw, 1997 Ironman Europe Champion, comforted me during the whole ordeal. Seeing that I'd be fine, she soon departed to finish her ride and I got it together to start riding home. Well, with all the distractions in the form of traveling I'd had during my Ironman training, I didn't want to lose more quality riding time, so I put in another 60 miles followed by a four-mile run.

When I got home, I jumped into the shower and with the water stinging me all over, my Body had only one thing to say: "Idiot!"

With more misfortune to follow, six days later I sent this one, titled *News Flash:*

This just in: Legendary bonehead cyclist Paul Martin is at it again. Just days after his notorious "Body Retaliates" crash, Martin eats it on his road bike for an unprecedented seventh time in a single season.

Our reporter on the scene, Heebee Bummin, has the report:

It appears that Mr. Martin was last in a line of three riders descending a hill on a sharp right hand turn when a large dog and its owner were walking up the inside lane of the blind corner, in the opposite direction. The first two riders veered to safety, but Martin, his options lessened by the others, had no choice but to go down. And down he went on the shady, gravel-strewn corner.

A witness on the scene, incidentally, the owner of the driveway whose gravel was in the road and towards whom we understand Martin holds no grudge—only because he supplied the necessary first-aid kit—commented, "You know it's a bad crash when the guy's leg pops off!"

Dr. Susan Latshaw, attending physician, lent these words, "There are two kinds of people in this world. Paul's the type that likes to dance with gravity."

Paul's Body was unavailable for comment, apparently on a much-needed long weekend.

As the group was preparing to finish the 100-mile ride, Martin was overheard in a display of sick, masochistic humor: "Let's hit the road!"

Thank you, Heebee.

Martin was admitted to a local clinic for a tetanus shot and gravel removal. We are told the pea-size hole in his hip should close up in a few days.

In a related story, a recent poll suggests that America's fear of amputees is at an all-time high.

Whether I'm driving, skiing or cycling, I clearly have some type of self-preservation deficit. When the time comes for me to travel with the wife and kids—if and when I have them—I think I'll let my wife drive. A few weeks after that e-mail, sufficiently healed from the latest mishap, I had the opportunity to speak to seventh graders at Parker Vista West Middle School in Denver's southern suburbia. After the appearance, I received another bundle of letters from students attending my presentation. One letter in particular stood out from the rest.

Dear Paul Martin,

How are you? I'm writing to you because I would like to thank you for coming and talking at our school. You made me realize how much I appreciate what I have. You also made me realize that I can get to my goal in life if I try. My goal in life is to become a singer. Singing is my gift and that is what I'm going to strive for, and I am going to make it. You made such an impact in my life and I don't know how to thank you. This may seem like just a small letter that 149 other kids are going to write, but it's not, you've changed my life.

> *Your Friend,*
> *Kira Waite*

Speaking to kids pays the rent; receiving letters...priceless!

The Hawaiian Ironman remained my focus, and in early September of 1998 I began tapering for the biggest race in triathlon.

When one trains for an endurance event, it is immensely important to taper before race day. This refers to cutting down on training mileage and intensity for a specific period, depending on the length of the upcoming race, to provide ample time for the body to rest and repair itself in preparation for optimal performance. One final race remained before I could pull back on the throttle.

Three weeks before Ironman, the IPC staged its Cycling World Championships for the Disabled in Colorado Springs. Athletes from around the globe came to race. I had qualified for Team USA with my results at cycling nationals earlier that summer.

The altitude and terrain in Colorado Springs were similar to my training grounds in Boulder and were less than 90 miles to the south. This gave me a tremendous advantage. The race consisted of four laps of a nine-mile course, mostly hills, ranging from 7,400 to 9,000 feet above sea level, on the grounds of the United States Air Force Academy. Much of that course was covered in the 1988 (able-bodied) Cycling World Championships.

Dory and Gary were my teammates. Dory was more of a sprinter and short distance time trialist than a hill climber, so we anticipated that the lead pack would drop him early in the race, leaving Gary and me to battle the favored Europeans. Through two laps, most of the competitors stayed together. Near the top of the first hill, the major climb, the French rider Patrice Ceria attacked and broke away as Czech Jiri Jezek and I took chase. We rode at near maximum effort for about a minute before the three of us rode alone in a breakaway; it was clear that no one would bridge the gap if we held an aggressive pace.

Passing by the starting line, the feed zone (where a team's staff members hand out water bottles as needed) and the finish line area (where coaches and supporters gather), I couldn't contain my excitement as I was anticipating a first, second or third place finish in a world championship event. I sang the popular string of lyrics from James Brown's *I Got You (I Feel Good)* as I passed my supporters. After the race, friends commented on how fresh I looked each time I passed. The truth was, I felt so good about the progressing race that the pain I was experiencing in my lungs and legs took a back seat.

The game plan, had Gary been with the pack near the end, was for me to attack with a half mile to go. In the event that I could not hold the lead through the finish line, he would use his decades of race wisdom to manipulate a strategic sprint to win the race. Since Gary wasn't around, I followed a modified game plan and broke away at the half-mile-to-go point.

Similar to the nationals, the finish line was 200 meters from the crest of the final 200-meter, nine percent grade. When I reached the start of the climb, some 30 to 40 meters ahead of the others, I felt myself fading and opted to hold back and climb with them, hoping to out-sprint them to the finish. Halfway up the hill, Patrice attacked aggressively while Jiri and I gazed at each other in disbelief and conceded to a battle for second and third. As we crested the hill, we broke into an all-out sprint for the finish line that stretched out over 30 seconds. My inexperience revealed itself as I held the windward side and the Czech crept ahead in my draft zone and bettered me by half a bike length! Very exciting stuff.

After the race, my breakaway partners told me that they had each conceded the win to me when I took off near the end, and, had I kept hammering, the race would have been mine.

Ride, live and learn.

Three days later, I packed my bags and departed for the Big Island of Hawaii for The Big Race—The Ironman.

The Hawaiian Ironman

The Ironman is often described as an event instead of a race. Many of the athletes on the island were not there to chase an age-group title. They were there to make it to the finish line and brag about it for the rest of their lives. I arrived a week before the race ready to win—I'm a little competitive. In my category, the physically challenged, there was one other BK amputee and three wingers, one of them female. I was there to beat them and as many four-limbed freaks as I could.

Such goals require training, and lots of it. In my own nine-week program I had managed eight 100-mile bike rides, most of them solo, and 60 miles in the pool, but, unfortunately, not too many miles running— only 102 total. Stumpie was having problems.

Nearly every other aspect of my Ironman preparation was in order: plenty of rest during training, proper nutrition and the anxious feeling to get started. I had no reason to be afraid, no reason to be anything but confident. (If there was one thing I would have changed about my virgin Ironman experience, it would be the dirt and dead bugs in my condo. It's true that you get what you pay for.) The bottom line: I was ready to race.

Throughout the week, the energy was slowly building in the small town of Kona, as Saturday's race approached. More and more athletes gathered on the pier each morning to share stories about qualifying races and training schedules. All the big names were in town. I met Luc Van Lierde, the 1996 overall winner, at the Lava Java coffee shop early in the week. On another day, I exchanged hellos by the water with Cam Widoff, the first American finisher in 1997 and a fellow Boulderite. I caught a water bottle Wendy Ingraham tossed to the crowd during the Parade of Nations. In the parade, the athletes grouped with their fellow countrymen to march down Ali'i Drive in the center of Kona in a display of patriotism. I chose not to walk because I didn't want to give Stumpie any unnecessary aggravation before the race.

The event organizers even made a big deal out of Thursday night's carbo-loading pasta dinner before the race. Bob Babbitt, the guy who told the San Diego Challenge Triathlon participants that I'd be breaking Ironman records someday, emceed the pre-race production and got us all fired up for the Big Day.

Finally, it was Friday night. I was itching for the cannon blast that would signify the start of the race the next morning. Strangely, unlike any other night before any other race I'd ever done, I fell asleep early and didn't wake until the alarm sounded at 4:15 a.m.

Saturday, October 3, 1998. Race Day. I made myself a four-egg omelet with a toasted PBJ and a cup o' Joe, just like I had every other day that week.

I arrived at the pier at 5:45 a.m. I'd racked my bike the day before. I gave things a final check. All was in order. There were no surprises.

At 6:50 a.m. I entered the water for an exceptionally brief warm-up and set myself up near the boat that marked the left side of the starting line—about 75 meters wide—one third of the way back in the pack. Karen Smyers, the 1995 women's champion, had given some free tips one night earlier in the week and she mentioned that lining up left would eliminate some of the flailing arms during the swim and would only add about five meters to the total swim distance. I figured that should work for me, being a relatively weak swimmer.

Everyone was so anxious in those preceding moments. You could almost pick out the rookies. They were all doing what I was doing— looking around, wondering what everyone else was doing.

The cannon blast does not necessarily go off at 7 a.m. sharp, but when everyone's all settled in. It could be coming in a minute, or in two minutes, or any second…

BOOM! The mighty cannon fired. It was Show Time!

The mad rush for position was nowhere near as violent as I had expected. It seemed I had picked a good place to start. There weren't too many people passing me. I was not getting clobbered. I felt comfortable.

Then, go figure, a minor problem arose about 10 minutes into the swim—my right goggle kept filling up with water. I'd worn the goggles for two months without a glitch. I flipped on my back and emptied it—in the midst of all those flailing arms—but it filled back up immediately. I tried again with no luck. I had to complete nearly the entire 2.4 mile swim with one eye closed.

I reached the halfway point of the swim in a little over 35 minutes. It took 36 minutes to get back to the pier.

With about a half mile to go, I saw Randy Caddell, one of the paraplegic wheelchair competitors, swimming alongside me. We swam together for a little while but he must have been pushing hard for the finish because he exited the water nearly a minute ahead of me.

I had hoped for a 1:15 swim and got out in just under 1:12. Richard, my race-appointed "handler," was right there for me at the ramp. We grabbed each other and I hopped about 20 feet to the chair where he'd set up my bike leg. A quick clothing change in the tent, a 30-meter trip to the bike, and there were three volunteers, holding my bike and strapping on my heart rate monitor for me. I was riding less than five minutes after I'd exited the water. Impressive.

As I took the corner, exiting the pier, I saw the huge crowd on hand and my energy soared. It was awesome. Total strangers were calling my name, and for the first time ever I felt a bit like a celebrity. (I believed in my pseudo-celebrity status for the next nine months, before it was brought to my attention that the names of all competitors are called out on the P.A. system as they exit the bike transition.)

I felt great on the way out, at least for a little while. For the first 20 miles or so I was riding at around 21 m.p.h. That was before the winds arrived. At about Mile 35 on the bike, the gusts felt like they were pushing 50 m.p.h.

I rode with many of the same people in several sections along the course. We would see one another for an hour or so, then split up for the rest of the ride. Dave and Bob, two athletes I had met that week, caught me after about an hour on the bike. Dave went by me first, then Bob caught up and passed me minutes later. It felt great to realize that I had beaten them both out of the water.

The grind up to the spectator-packed little island village of Hawi was a rough one. The wind was pounding me in the face all the way up the incline. It took me three hours and five minutes on the bike to get to the turnaround there in Hawi.

The race marshals issued three-minute penalties for the first drafting or blocking offense, and a disqualification for the second. I was a tad paranoid and very careful not to break the rules for the entire ride.

The return trip offered a 10-mile flat section with a strong and beautiful tailwind. But more side winds and headwinds followed. I reached the bike/run transition three hours and five minutes from the turnaround in Hawi, the same time it took me to get there. I was thinking that the way back would be considerably faster because of two or three sections of tailwind, but the return was a few more miles than the way out and I wasn't hitting it quite so hard. The last 35 miles or so I backed off, knowing the run would require some legs. (In retrospect, I think I could have pushed a little harder on the bike. But I have no regrets; I believe I did the right thing in the face of unknown territory.)

My poorly calibrated bike computer added extra aggravation. I didn't realize it was inaccurate until I got back to town. With several miles still remaining, it already read 112. This alone made the final miles tougher than they needed to be.

The bike ride took its toll on three friends of mine: Keith Ballard, Cavlin Curnutte (fellow BK) and Susan Latshaw. Keith was coasting into the entrance of the second transition when I caught up to him. This transition, T2 in tri lingo, was located at the Kona Surf Hotel, several miles south of the pier. He had a not-so-comfortable look on his face when I passed him. I later learned he was in a big hurt and had to stay in T2 for three hours. He only made it 13 miles into the run before dropping out of the race.

Calvin didn't finish either. He made it through 68 miles on the bike and had to bail. He told me later that at that point he was out of steam and looking for a sign as to whether or not he should continue the fight.

Just then a big gust of wind nearly blew him off his bike, and he decided to pull over and wait for a ride back to Kona.

Susan, my occasional riding partner back in Boulder, had dropped out due to a chronic foot injury.

I had another relatively quick transition and was off the bike and on the run course in less than five minutes. As I exited the dressing room, I heard someone calling my name from the left and looked over to see Susan. I felt badly that she'd had to drop out, but it was so great to see her. I was feeling extremely positive overall and she added a little something by being there to see me off. It must have had something to do with her professional triathlete status. She helped me feel like a part of the tri-community, like I belonged there.

I opted to walk up the 100-meter hill at the start of the run. Then, just as I fell into a trot, I entered the infamous Pit, located immediately south of transition. After I'd descended the relatively steep, 150-meter hill, I walked most of the way out of it. At this early stage of the run, a competitor's legs are still in cycling mode, which makes both the descent and subsequent hill climb much more difficult than they would normally be.

The crowd's energy picked up at the intersection of Ali'i Drive and Ali'i Highway, at about Mile 1.5. I started to feel really good, that is to say, better than expected. I'd hoped for nine-minute miles for a good part of the run.

As I headed into town at around Mile 8, the generous crowd continued with the "Go Paul!" chants. I still couldn't believe how many people knew my name. My ignorance was a huge advantage.

Among the spectators, I saw Jim Howley just before town. The sight of him gave me tremendous positive energy, taking away some of the all-consuming pain. My entire body was feeling the effects from the windy ride: my neck and shoulders hurt, I had a bit of a headache and my legs were as heavy as I expected them to be at the start of the marathon. In any endurance event, familiar faces always help you to refocus.

Climbing Pay & Save Hill—named for the grocery store alongside it—was the highlight of the day to that point. There were still lots of "Go

Paul!" cries from the crowd and tons of new energy. I couldn't help smiling as I facetiously asked everyone to please move to the Queen Ka'ahumanu Highway, where the roadside would surely be empty and desolate, for further support. The majority of the bike and run portions of the race are staged on the Queen K along the western shore of the island. The road is feared by competitors because of its windy ride and hot, steaming run.

The Queen wasn't too much of an antagonist that day. The sky was overcast for most of the run, so the notorious heat was not a major problem. I'd been drinking plenty of Race Day—the energy drink supplied by the organizers at all aid stations—and eating plenty of Balance Bar Minis and Gu. I think I nailed the diet really well. I didn't hit The Wall all day and felt properly nourished.

I walked at a few aid stations and stopped at several to pull off the leg to relieve some of the discomfort. Midway through the marathon, I learned the benefits of pouring ice water all over Stumpie to cool him off and numb him up just enough to take the edge off. Ahhh, each time I did, the next mile was so much more comfortable.

I ever-so-thankfully reached the run turnaround at the Natural Energy Lab—an actual scientific research laboratory—feeling strong. The Lab turned out to be a wonderful energy provider. Getting to the entrance was a huge mental hurdle; reaching the beginning of the end removed any doubts about whether or not I would finish the race. Going into the Lab, I told myself, "When I get out, I'm only a 10k away. Standard stuff." Plus, before me was the first good descent in a while. I passed more people there than anywhere else on the run.

At Mile 18, I realized that if I kept a steady pace, I'd cross the line in under 12 hours. I had pretty much been on that pace for the entire run. The first couple of miles were at a 10-minute pace with the early walking, and then I picked it up to a nine-minute pace for the next eight to 10 miles. The long steady hill on the Queen K had me doing a couple 11-minute miles. I chanted the words to Black Sabbath's *Ironman*, both in my head and aloud, over and over along the run, along with my new standard, "I feel good...da duhna duhna duh...I knew that I would now ...da duhna duhna duh." Somehow, a little song helps keep my head steady.

I was picking up the pace toward the end of Queen K, where volunteers were passing out glow sticks to runners headed in the other direction as they set out upon the unlit highway. It is considered something of a victory to complete the race before dusk and earn the name "daytime finisher." The glow stick hanging around your neck generally designates that you did not reach this internal goal. Dusk settled in as I hit the top of the hill near Mile 24. The streets were lit at that point and there was no way in hell I was going to accept the offered glow stick. I passed on it to attain my own version of a daytime finish.

I saw more spectators when I reached the top of the last hill, a tough one. I knew that once I reached the crest, it would literally be all downhill from there, beginning with the descent of Pay & Save Hill. There weren't nearly as many people lined up along the hill on the way down as there had been on the way up. They were all cheering at the finish line.

My good friend Joel Sampson, a BK triathlete I had raced in Toledo, emerged from the crowd and started running with me. Paranoia about receiving any type of assistance that might result in a penalty crept in and I asked him to please back off. Pure paranoia.

A little stretch of the Kua'kini Highway, at the base of Pay & Save Hill, was mentally the longest section of the race. I could see and hear the finish as I descended the hill, but then I had to turn south on the Kua'kini. It was such a tease to be running away from the finish line. It's probably less than a quarter of a mile to the drop down to Ali'i Drive, but it felt so much farther.

As I descended that little hill, the crowd was getting louder and louder. I kept seeing more and more spectators as I picked up speed. Then I turned right onto Ali'i Drive, the most famous street in all of triathlon. The road was lit and the I-just-did-Ironman! feeling was starting to overcome me. The floodlight over the finish line structure seemed auspicious...and I cracked a little smile. There it was in all its glory, the finish of the Hawaiian Ironman. Holy grail-like. I kicked it in for the last hundred yards and gave the "Raise the Roof" signal in the process. The crowd roared.

Eleven hours, 55 minutes, and 37 seconds after the cannon blasted, I leapt onto the finish line in classic conquering style. I asked my catchers to step back a bit as I pulled off my leg, raising it to the crowd on the left, proclaiming in my best Ozzy Osbourne style: "I...AM...IRONMAN!" I then turned to offer the leg to the stands on the right and let out a howl. The crowd was on its feet. Majestic. What an incredibly powerful moment!

My catchers tried to usher me out of the corral as I pumped my fists to the crowd to share my happiness. The photo flashes were going off and the NBC cameraman was right in my face. I locked eyes with Jim Howley at the top of the stands as I pointed to the clock with conviction. He nodded his head, well aware of what I had just done. I was so full of joy, completion and self-esteem.

It was the happiest moment I had ever experienced.

I finally left the corral and headed toward the finisher medal line. I kept telling the catchers how happy I was but I think they already knew. I was, surprisingly, feeling strong, fully aware of my surroundings and in no need of outside assistance. My brain had shut off all the pain long enough for me to enjoy the moment.

As I stood in line for my medal, I saw Dr. Rob DeStefano, the chiropractor who gave me my first swimming lesson and triathlon training program. He was clearly pleased to have witnessed my climb from a one-lap huffer and puffer to an Ironman finisher. I was so glad he was there.

He was not there to race but to administer chiropractic work and a muscle-healing procedure known as the Active Release Technique. He had raced Ironman Canada just a month ago in a time of 12:05. (Ten minutes slower than my time, so, of course, I rubbed it in at the awards ceremony the next night.)

I began to cry as several random people congratulated me. They asked if I was all right. I assured them that I couldn't have been happier.

I walked over to the edge of the pier and sat looking out at the water I had climbed into 12 hours earlier. I shed a few more tears, accompanied by a slight smile. I thanked Everything for helping me complete an Ironman.

Then I headed over for a 45-minute massage, complete with chicken soup and rolls. Kimberly, my masseuse du jour, even gave Stumpie a little work. He was hurtin'.

After my massage, I went back to the finish line to look for friends, any friends, but I came up short. I wanted to share my race with somebody. I wanted to relive the whole thing again right there.

I decided to take up Kimberly's offer to meet her and a friend at Quinn's for a celebratory beer and some grub. She'd been warned that I had no money but seemed happy to provide. I had a burger and a Sam Adams and relished every mouthful.

The girls were kind enough to give me a ride home and even picked up some ice for Stumpie. They came into the condo and set me up with the ice pack before departing. After a quick shower, I crawled into bed, exhausted. The post-race excitement kept my head racing for a couple of more hours. I finally fell asleep around 3 a.m.

In the morning, I was swollen and sore all over. My back was hurting. My foot was hurting. My whole right leg was bummin'. And Stumpie was in no condition to walk. I somehow obtained a pair of crutches—what a blessing they were. I moved very slowly but managed to cross the street to Jolly Rogers, where a wonderful stack of pancakes eased the pain.

I met up with a couple of friends later in the day and we made our way to a pre-awards party. There I met Tim DeBoom and his wife, Nicole, both professional triathletes and Boulderites. Tim, despite coming in tenth overall, was a bit bummed. He had completed a great race but was kicked on the swim and suffered two chipped teeth and a slight concussion. (He would come back in 1999 to place third; in 2000 he would finish second; in 2001 he would win the race—and $70,000!)

Outside the awards dinner, Roch Frey (pronounced "Rock Fry" not "Roach Free") and his wife, 1997 winner Heather Fuhr, came over to congratulate me. I must say, when the sport's finest coach and a former champion go out of their way to offer kind words, you can't help but feel good. I had followed Roch's off-the-shelf Ironman training program to prepare for the race. Apparently, it had worked.

The awards started, and soon it was time for the physically challenged category. Clarinda Brueck, the arm amputee who founded the International Triathlon Union's Physically Challenged Division, received her award, then John Santana—an arm amputee and native Hawaiian—then me. The presenters gave each of the challenged finishers a trophy and a special edition stainless steel Timex Ironman watch. I accepted mine, then took my place to the right of the others. Smiling broadly toward the crowd, I raised my crutches and crossed them over my head. The crowd went nuts and seconds later we were receiving a standing ovation. Once again, I was in my glory and loving it.

We exited, stage left, but not before I dropped the trophy in front of everybody. If you can't laugh at yourself…

As I chatted it up with the VIPs, an attractive young woman approached me, quite enthusiastically, and asked if she could take a picture with me. I graciously accepted. I was talking with Dr. Rob at the time, and we gave each other the "Hey, look at me/Hey, look at you" glance as I put my arm around her for a pose before walking back to my seat to check out my fancy new watch.

Then they announced the top professional female finishers. This year's winner, Swiss sedentary receptionist Mom-turned-super-endurance-athlete, Natasha Badmann, gave an emotional acceptance speech that went on and on about the warm water and how good it felt. She said that when she hit the headwinds on the bike she spread her wings to fly. Deep stuff. Then the professional men's winner, Peter Reid, graciously accepted his championship trophy.

On the way out, I ran into Lynn Brooks who, moments before, was given an Isuzu SUV—the official Ironman vehicle—for completing 19 consecutive races in Kona. She had said on stage that she wasn't even going to come to the awards since she wasn't feeling well. Then, total surprise, they'd given her a vehicle. She showed me her two-foot key and asked if I wanted to go for a ride.

I turned around, and there was Brazil's favorite triathlete, Fernanda Keller, congratulating me. She's known as one of the most physically attractive athletes in the sport, so of course I took the opportunity to congratulate her back with a kiss. She offered one cheek, then the other. I told her she was beautiful and headed on my way. I must have been nervous or star-struck or something because I couldn't remember if she smiled or reacted or anything.

We arrived at Lulu's, the post-party place to be. People were congratulating me from all sides. For a second, I could actually feel my head swelling. Dr. Rob was in the mix. He pulled me over to the bar where he set up his friends with a round of Cuervos. "Don't worry, I'm loaded," he said. I wasn't sure if he meant that he had a lot of money, a lot to drink, or both. We hung out there for the rest of the night and partied down like happy little Ironmen.

My experience in Hawaii was not unlike that of other rookie Ironman triathletes—magical. The struggle to keep moving and the resulting confirmation that I can push myself to extremes reminded me that I will forever be in control of my choices. Just a year and a half before I completed the original one-day extreme endurance event, I had laughed at the suggestion that I could attempt such a feat. But my father's long-ago words had convinced me: "I can do it because the other guy can do it."

All the athletes in Hawaii had arrived with an undefeatable spirit. They had a willingness to keep going, despite the pain. You might ask, "Why would they do that to themselves?"

For the feeling at the finish line, that's why. There's really nothing like it.

The Hawaiian Ironman: what an absolutely spectacular life-changing experience!

The Grass Isn't Always Greener

Sometimes we pursue goals with such vigor that we lose sight of our priorities. We become so focused on reaching the intended goal that when circumstances repeatedly suggest that a change of course is clearly in our best interest, we continue to miss the message. I often put myself in risky positions with this "never quit" attitude.

Such was the case with my pursuit of the National Ski Team. Limited success and lack of cohesion with the majority of the team members finally brought the message home that I should step away from the scene, at least temporarily. For several years running, a sub-standard ski season had followed a competitive summer athletic season filled with tremendous feelings of accomplishment and progress. Regardless, I had consistently approached each winter with fresh vigor. My work ethic and enjoyment of carving high-speed turns provided all the necessary motivation. But the solid season I had hoped for, one which would impress the national coaches, not merely sufficiently but enthusiastically, never materialized. It was the "merely sufficient" attitude that had prevailed when Herman and the staff eventually added my name to the roster.

With the Ironman behind me, the time came once again to focus on the sport of the season: alpine ski racing. The U.S. team's first on-snow training camp took place at Copper Mountain, Colorado, conveniently located less than two hours from Boulder.

Becoming a member of the "C" team had taken three years of hard work, dedication and sacrifice. Almost immediately after being named to the squad, I felt an anticlimactic sentiment about the honor. With the exception of a few members, the team did not have the anticipated work ethic and athleticism I sought so long ago when I left New Jersey and the corporate world. From my early days on snow, many aspects of the team left me longing for a more dedicated "national" attitude among my teammates and myself. I had seen these signs early in my pursuit of team status, but ignored them for fear of losing interest. Clear thinking aside, I had told myself that I would make the team, so I had to make the team. I assumed that entry into this elite group would justify all of the negatives encountered during the quest.

A slew of debilitating minor injuries in the 1998-99 ski season led me to admit to myself that I should focus on endurance sports. I suffered a pulled tendon in Stumpie from training on a leg press, rendering my prosthetic unwearable. Two weeks later, I broke my prosthetic ski leg at a race in Park City, Utah—the same race at which I had broken my shoulder the year before. The race leg was repaired and I had the prosthetist include a minor redesign in the ankle to make it stronger.

Unfortunately, the modified finished product contained a structural misalignment. This change in alignment caused the leg to react differently in certain circumstances, which, in turn, required time to master. But time was running out. Only five days remained before our trip to Europe for the World Cup events.

Because of my infinite lack of common sense, I approached the first day on the new leg—after waiting a week for the repair to be completed—in reckless fashion. That morning was midway through a 10-day speed camp at Purgatory, Colorado, during which the other team members had already completed sufficient inspection runs down the fast course in preparation for all-out race training. My first run led to a careless, injury-free crash. The second run, despite catching 120 feet of "air" (distance, not height) off a mid-course roll, was without incident. The third, however, ended in a crash so severe that I missed the next few days of training.

Barreling down the hill at nearly 40 m.p.h. and closing in on the bottom, I came off a slight roll in such a way that my skis kicked out to the right and I totally lost control. I landed on my left hip, which over the next three days turned deeper and deeper shades of purple. The bruise eventually made its way around my lower abdomen until the base of my penis turned black and blue. Now that's a crash.

My performances at the European World Cup races in the following weeks were sub-par, to say the least. I had missed several days of desperately needed training, I was sporting a leg that I wasn't comfortable skiing on and I was competing on the most difficult race courses that I had ever had the displeasure to descend. I delivered lackluster performances in both the Swiss and Austrian Alps. Furthermore, I was still suffering from the hip injury. The team doctors had drained 60 ccs of fluid from it the night before the first downhill training run in Anzére, Switzerland.

Back in Breckenridge for the World Cup Finals a couple of weeks after our trip, I suffered an exceptionally painful bout of folliculitis—an infected hair follicle on Stumpie located in a weight-bearing area. It might sound harmless, but try walking on one. That kept me off skis for a few days and forced me to miss the downhill, my favorite race.

Accompanying my poor attitude was my energy-draining financial status. Despite receiving several large sums in recent weeks (William E. Simon Olympic Endowment, $5,000; the Challenged Athlete Foundation grant, $2,250; Ironman media incentive payments from Balance Bar, $4,000), I was continually broke and stressed about paying rent, bills and the multitude of costs associated with being an all-season professional-amateur athlete. The last straw was probably the fact that, even after receiving this latest set of checks and paying back a large portion of the loans I had accumulated with friends and family, my net debt held steady at $30,000.

The big sponsorship I was led to believe would be in place by now from NovaCare, the largest national prosthetic provider in the country, would be continually delayed until the company was bought by Hangar Prosthetics. The previous December, I had met with the company liaison, who had told me the paperwork was in place and ready to sign. She explained, quite candidly, that I would receive $1,000 for every race I entered whether able-bodied or disabled, triathlon or skiing, finish or no finish. I expressed my surprise and commented that I raced at least two or three weekends every month. She said they would all be eligible as paid performances.

I almost couldn't believe it. The deal, which had already been 12 months in the making, sounded far too good to be true. The paperwork was in her hotel room and she was going to present it to me for review in the morning.

I never saw her again. I later learned of the buyout by Hangar, which occurred a month afterward, and I concluded that this was the reason for my abandonment.

I had quite literally banked on that contract with my creditors— friends and family—for the past year. It was the type of sponsorship I had envisioned when I quit my job with Lincoln Electric. The promising vision was suddenly washed away and my hopes for a continued full-time commitment, the only way to be the best at my chosen endeavors, were fading.

I informed a good friend that I was close to a decision to go back to work and forget about my athletic dreams. I explained to Tabi King that if I were to go to work, I wouldn't do it half-heartedly. My "real" job would be my priority and athletic competition would take a back seat; more than likely it would be dropped altogether.

Thankfully, Tabi brought my vision back into focus by convincing me—reminding me—that I had a very unique product to offer: myself. I knew how to sell myself and she had always seen that. I had a hook and I'd be stupid not to use it.

"Make a workout video, be a speaker, write a book. You are so very marketable. Do something with it!" she told me. I took her advice and decided I would put training and competition on the back burner after ski season to reassess my priorities.

Near the end of my rookie season on the National Ski Team, at a race just south of Reno, Nevada, I unwittingly accelerated my own plan and retired from the team.

I was not in good graces with Herman, the head coach who took offense to my occasional commentary on the state of certain team issues.

Adding fuel to his fire, I was sometimes tardy in meeting my financial obligations to the team. At a brief meeting preceding the day's super-G race, he became perhaps the only person to ever call me a "whiner" with conviction.

A misunderstanding had left me ignorant of the monies due for lodging at the hotel in Reno, which I thought were complimentary from the resort. This, plus my own irresponsibility in not directly informing him that I would be unable to attend the previous day's awards ceremony, gave him reason to suspend me from further races until the balance was paid. (Several weeks earlier I had committed to a fashion photo shoot with *We Media* magazine, a disabled lifestyle publication. It was my first—and last—paid modeling gig.)

At that very instant I decided, finally, to commit my energies toward triathlon and cycling. When I told him of my decision, he stood up and walked away. I continued speaking to the back of his head. I don't think he even heard me.

I left the hill, and as I headed to my car with a set of skis on each shoulder, I saw Herman. Our eyes met and I gave him a little wave goodbye.

"See ya," he responded coldly, sufficiently sealing my departure. I forwarded my formal written resignation a week later.

When I got back to the hotel that morning, I headed directly to the shower and shaved my legs. I was a triathlete again.

In the summer of 1997, I had been issued a faulty equipment traffic ticket in New York City for a broken headlight. The headlight was fixed within 24 hours, and the appropriate paperwork was sent to the proper precinct. Six months later, back in Boulder, I received notification that my license would be suspended in 30 days if I didn't pay the $60 ticket. Irresponsibility on my end led me to pay the fine several days late.

My license was suspended and the long arm of the law (a stop sign) eventually caught up with me. Colorado law mandates five days in the county jail for driving on a suspended license. After my case had spent nearly a year in the courts, Judge Cecil Williams of the Grand County Courthouse sentenced me to spend five days in jail, to be served at the end of the ski season.

Since my ski season ended sooner than expected, I called the jail superintendent and checked in three weeks early. I was ready to take Tabi's advice and write a book. A short stint in a quiet jail without many distractions would provide the right environment. Once again, opportunity had presented itself in the guise of adversity.

Recommitment

My stint in the Big House passed rather quickly. My eagerness to begin my story kept me focused for five or six hours a day. I also checked into the joint with an athletic goal—to do 2,500 push-ups before I checked out. I completed the task with the help of "push-up poker." Instead of dollars, the wagers involve push-ups. A typical loss at the end of a round would cost you about 30 to 40 of 'em. I left my confinement stronger, ready to be an athlete again and carried by the momentum of an autobiography-in-progress. Good stuff.

A reborn confidence in my abilities brought a new and stronger desire to proceed as an athlete. The Paralympics were still out there. The sub-10:30 Ironman was out there. The sub-3:15 marathon was out there. I had left my job four years earlier with a goal, and it involved more than earning a spot on the U.S. Disabled Ski Team. It was a commitment to myself to make a living doing whatever it was I felt passionate about at the time.

My entry into the whole mission was undoubtedly the prosthetic leg. I am very passionate about my ability to compete in endurance sports with some of the best able-bodied athletes out there, lately in the top 10 percent. (My best finish amongst ABs as of this writing is 11th out of 251 in my age group.) While I believe I could have made it to the professional ranks as an able-bodied triathlete, the truth is, I most likely wouldn't have walked that path. Without my fortuitous accident, I might have continued a struggle up the corporate ladder with Lincoln Electric or I might have ended up working for their competition. Maybe I would have joined the Peace Corps for all I know. Frankly, I'm not the least bit concerned with how my life would have turned out had I not lost my leg. I only know that I wouldn't go back in time and change things even if I could. I am happy being an amputee with no money, being "fiscally challenged." The perpetual empty wallet is a constant source of stress but I look at it this way: I'm just another starving student working toward a doctorate. Mine will be in *Paulrobertmartinology:* the study of myself.

I was not yet finished. Early in my one-legged athletic career, I had hoped to earn an invitation to the Atlanta Paralympics as a runner. That never happened. I tried to make it to the Nagano Paralympics as an alpine ski racer, but failed to do so. Now I decided to attempt to compete in the Sydney Paralympic Games as a cyclist. If I reached this goal, would I be finished? Who knew?

A great sponsorship opportunity came up in the summer of '99. The Walnut Brewery in Boulder crafted a batch of beer especially for me called Finish Line Rye. Talk about an honor. My own beer! A portion of the brew's sales were used to finance some of my ever-present race expenses.

I had created a friendship with the folks at Schwinn, headquartered in Boulder, and they graciously set me up with road and mountain bikes. The new race bike arrived that summer just in time to allow me to sell the old one for rent money. (A couple of years later I would be riding a Griffen Vulcan—a boron carbide rocket ship—and be sponsored by B&L Bike and Sport.) Brooks Sports, makers of shoes and apparel, was also extremely supportive. They not only provided all the running gear I needed, but they financed many of my races and student presentations, and eventually set me up with a monthly stipend to help me focus on Sydney. Funny, a running company helped me focus on cycling.

TEC Interface Systems, manufacturers of prosthetic socket components, provided both comfort and a competitive edge for my run leg. After a short period running on Springlite feet, my latest walk and run pylons came, once again, from Flex-Foot.

My recommitment anchored itself right off the bat. I raced in several national calendar triathlons and a few bike races in 1999 and kept my thoughts on Sydney.

Of the 1,200 competitors at St. Anthony's Triathlon, an Olympic distance race (1.5k swim, 40k bike and 10k run) in St. Petersburg, Florida, the physically challenged athletes were the first to enter the water. I came out of the water in second place, behind AK amputee Brian Leske. I caught him on the bike and came into the run transition behind the flashing blue and red lights of the police pace car. The crowd ignited, not expecting one of the PC athletes to still be holding the lead. That lead lasted 2.5 miles into the run before a 19-year-old able-bodied speedster passed me. Dad, his girlfriend Lillian, and my sister Paty were there to witness my finish time of two hours, 22 minutes. I was the 22nd competitor to cross the line.

At the 1999 Disabled Cycling Nationals, Gary Seghi beat me in the time trial by less than 20 seconds on the 40-kilometer course. The following day he suffered the same problems as he had the year before. He crashed into another rider who had gone down in front of him. Seeing an opportunity, and with 13 miles left in the 39-mile road race, I took off like a man possessed. To insure a win, I knew I had to take advantage of his misfortune. That 13-mile stretch inspired perhaps the hardest effort I have ever put forth on a bike. The motorcycle officiating the race fed me lead times of 45 seconds, then one minute, then a minute and a half, then three. I held my pace until two miles from the finish, when I felt comfortable that I would win. A certain amount of guilt accompanied my victory that day, but it was the right thing to do. Ask any bike racer.

The following week, members of the 1998 Cycling World Championship team were invited to Blois, France, to take part in the European Disabled Cycling Championships. In my first 32 years I had not set foot on the European continent, yet in the last six months I had traveled there to race for two different teams in two very different sports.

Blois had a beautiful "old world" feel to it. The narrow downtown streets tangled in the shadows of the Chateau du Blois, a castle whose history reaches back to the year 500. The castle's construction was completed in the 1600s.

The cycling races in Blois included both track and road events. I was not yet racing on the track—the velodrome—and the road events were being held late in the week. This gave me the time and freedom to leisurely enjoy various cafés along the Loire River in the old city. For several days I sat and read *Conversations With God, Book 3*, the last of a spiritual trilogy I had started a year before.

Road racing was still foreign to me. At that point, I had competed in less than a half dozen "pack" events, as opposed to individual time trials, so I approached this race with a focus on learning. Still, I remained hopeful for a strong showing and didn't rule out a possible win. Perhaps my time-trialing power would make up for my lack of strategic savvy.

Nope.

On the six-mile per lap, seven-lap course, Jiri Jezek shared my enthusiasm and we attacked the peloton three or four times each. Still feeling strong on the fifth lap, I pulled the lead pack up the grade on the course's one significant hill. Near the top, Jiri got out of his saddle to push the remaining 50 meters. Nearing exhaustion, and no longer feeling strong, I stayed seated and failed to get onto the back of the pack of six or seven cyclists that was following Jiri. I figured I would catch up with them over the roll.

There were three other riders in our lagging pack: Daniel Polson, a strong Australian rookie who later crashed attempting a high-speed corner; Gotfried Müller, the German reigning time trial world champion; and an unknown Frenchman. With these guys riding with me, I assumed that bridging the gap wouldn't be much of a problem. That was my critical judgment mistake of the day.

Among the things I learned that day were the importance of teammates and of selflessness in cycling. The others in my secondary pack each had a teammate in the lead peloton. Because Gary didn't make the trip and Dory had opted not to compete in the road race, I was the only U.S. rider on the course. With the peloton 100 meters in front of us, I was repeatedly covering about a third of the gap and rotating out to let one of the others assist in the effort to bridge. Each time I fell back our speed dropped to a soft pedal and we lost what I had just gained. I kept getting up front to close a third of the gap, only to be continually frustrated by the others' lack of effort. Having completed one full lap in this fashion,

I realized it was going to take a solo effort to win the race.

The strategy of the others remained a mystery to me until after the race, when someone took the time to explain it: the cyclists riding with me wanted their team to win, not necessarily themselves. "Oooohhhhh. I get it." Each of them knew I had the potential to win the race if I caught up to their teammates. These experienced riders knew that sitting back and letting me do all the work would squander my chances—Team USA's chances—at a victory.

It's safe to say their strategy worked. When I decided to chase the leaders without the help of the other three, I burned myself up in the process and dropped out of the race with one lap to go. The next day's time trial was going to be another all-out effort, and I knew that if I was to make a respectable showing, the only option, albeit a painful one, was to bow out of the road race.

Regarding the team concept: Daniel, the young Aussie, and I had made an informal pact the night before the road race. His teammate, Paul Lake, a terror on the track (who surprisingly went on to win the road race), was not expected to do well or even to finish the event. Paul is a big man and everyone, including him, thought the repeated hill would be too much for him and would prevent him from hanging on with the smaller, stronger climbers. Since we could each use a partner on the course, Daniel and I agreed to help each other if we could. As non-Europeans, neither of us was in contention for an official victory, so we would let the final sprint decide who should take the win if we were both in the mix.

Before the starting gun fired, Daniel's coach advised him to do what he had to do if his teammate, Paul Lake, was somehow in contention to win as the race developed. Daniel's lack of effort when I attempted to bridge the leaders left me wondering, *What the hell? I thought we had a deal?* He apologized up and down the next night for his empty words and actions. He repeatedly explained that he did what he was told. I understood. It was a team thing.

The guilt-ridden strategy to save myself for the next day paid off. On

Saturday, I rode the 17.5-kilometer course to a third place finish on my standard issue Schwinn Peloton road racing bike. Gotfried and Jiri took first and second, respectively, on their aerodynamically designed time trial bikes. Paul Lake came in 1.8 seconds behind me on his exclusive trial bike. A sweet, satisfying accomplishment indeed.

On Sunday the team traveled to Paris, where the majority boarded their flights back home. I opted to skip my flight for a chance to see Lance Armstrong win the Tour de France that afternoon.

Three team staff members and I took our spots on the Champs-Élysées—the main stage of the Tour adjacent to the Arc de Triomphe. I chose a tree branch 10 feet over the heads of 500,000 spectators to witness Lance and his U.S. Postal Service teammates (the Posties) ride to a victory in the world's most demanding and popular bike race—on a gorgeous sunny day. Later, the four of us fell asleep on the grass in a park facing the Eiffel Tower, each a victim of the previous night's celebratory antics. *Magnifique.*

A week later I was back in Boulder, where I raced in the Boulder Peak Triathlon. In the cycling portion of the event I beat several of the pro triathletes, including Scott Tinley, a two-time winner of the Hawaiian Ironman and one of the most popular and admired personalities in the sport. He later told me that I'd "better have beaten him" since he was coming off an illness and clearly hadn't put forth a typical effort. I didn't care why I'd beaten him. I was just glad I did.

But that was only on the bike. Scott more than made up for that on the swim and the run, and he beat me by over 20 minutes overall. The following week at the race that bears his name in Brian Head, Utah, there was no mistaking which one of us was the better triathlete. Healthy or not, that would be Mr. Tinley.

The Scott Tinley High Altitude Triathlon was one of the highest altitude races in the country. It was an off-road event—lake swim, mountain bike, trail run—and was the first of its kind for me. The 1,400-meter swim, at 8,400 feet, didn't take my breath away as I feared it would. The bike climb to the top of Brian Head, at 11,000 plus feet, was the killer. The strenuous pulling and twisting during the rocky ascent presented a subsequent level of challenge. I was having trouble with leg suspension, which forced me to stop and "reboot" six or seven times. Many of these reboots came at a time when I had to get off the bike and walk, because I could not ride several areas at my current skill level.

The crosswinds I experienced across the wide-open terrain while descending the mountain at 25 m.p.h. created nerve-racking conditions on the six-inch-wide single-track trail. The 19-mile ride took a lot out of me, adding two hours and 25 minutes onto my finishing time, and at the bottom of the hill, now at 9,400 feet, I still had a hilly 10k trail run to complete.

At one point early in the run, a hard-helmet-wearing lumberjack tried his best to stop me in the middle of the trail because his partner was about to fell a tree. I saw the unpleasant look in the partner's eyes when he was forced to delay his "Timber!" but I had a race to run and wasn't about to slow down for the sake of averting serious injury.

Mr. Tinley got the better of me on the bike that day by nearly 45 minutes, crossing the finish line minutes after I headed out on the run. Scott Tinley won, for the second time in as many years, the Second Annual Scott Tinley High Altitude Triathlon.

That race brought with it an unexpected accomplishment. I had set a goal for myself somewhere around 1997 to place in my age group in a USAT-sanctioned event before my days in triathlon were over. I did it. There were six competitors, including myself, in the 30-34 age group. The top guys clocked times of 3:41 and 3:44, respectively. My 3:51 was good enough for a third place podium finish.

It was time again for the ITU World Championships. This year the races were being held in Montreal in conjunction with the age-groupers and pros, like they were in Perth, Australia. Rivaldo Martins, who had beaten me fair and square in Perth but had had his medal stripped due to technicalities, was ready to battle for a legitimate World Championship.

But the Brazilian goofed again. As in Perth two years prior, he did not properly register for the race and was in jeopardy of losing his chance to compete in the physically challenged division. He personally petitioned Les MacDonald, president of the ITU, for a starting position. I happened to walk into the conversation and without even knowing what they were talking about, Les told me that Rivaldo would be racing the next day.

I'm very glad he did. There simply aren't enough challenged athletes competing in triathlon for the authorities to hold to rigid guidelines for qualification. Unfortunately, not everyone agrees with me on this issue. Rivaldo raced nonetheless.

He beat me out of the water by four minutes—much less damaging than the 11 minutes he had on me in Perth. I edged him on the bike by 30 seconds on the slick racecourse built for Formula One cars. It all came down to the run—triathlon *always* comes down to the run.

I ran my ass off, but I didn't run fast enough. My run times hadn't been particularly fast in the past two years due to prosthetic problems and because my focus had recently turned to cycling. Rivaldo added two more minutes to his lead on the 10k finishing leg of the race.

I went into the race hoping to break two hours, 15 minutes, which would be six minutes faster than my best time, and perhaps earn me the win. I finished with a new personal record of 2:15:26, a time I was very happy with. Rivaldo bettered me with his own PR of 2:09:09. Third place went to Ray Viscone, who broke the fibula in his good leg during the last 20 meters of the race. He crawled in on his hands and knees, seconds in front of Chase Baker, for the bronze honor. The race announcer let it be known that there was a wonderful photo opportunity happening. The next day's paper pictured Ray crawling across the finish line.

At the awards dinner the next night, I was asked to say a few words on behalf of Clarinda, our division founder who wasn't able to attend. After thanking those individuals who so graciously went out of their way to see that our division could have a successful and meaningful championship race, I delivered a personal "thank you" to Les MacDonald for allowing Rivaldo to race, saying, "I'd rather win a silver with him here than a gold without him." My desire for competition may have gotten the better of my judgment as I held the microphone speaking for the PC division, but I took advantage of the opportunity to voice my personal opinion. I think I was looking for a few "PC" points of my own.

The next big race on the agenda was the 1999 Hawaiian Ironman World Championships held annually in Kona. The race took place six weeks after the Montreal event.

My coach, Kathy Zawadzki, who also coached the U.S. Paralympic Cycling Team, combined Roch Frey's program with her own ideas to customize a program for me. During training, my solo 100-mile bike rides went well and strengthened my mental toughness. I also felt good on my long runs: 15-, 17- and 18-milers.

Three weeks before Ironman, I raced in San Diego at the U.S. Triathlon Series National Championships, which I intended to approach as a training day since it was all about Kona at that point.

The USTS race took quite an effort, beginning with the swim. The surf was so high that morning (10-foot faces!) that 50 of the 500 triathletes didn't even finish the opening discipline of the race. As I was finishing the swim, about 30 or 40 yards from the beach, I glanced back to see a tsunami rearing its ugly head some seven or eight feet above me. I took a deep breath, the frothy seawater nearly flipped my feet over my head, and just when I thought I couldn't hold my breath in anymore, I was plopped onto the sand.

I looked up and yelled for my Dad, who had orchestrated his RV tour to see me race in California, asking him to bring me my bike leg. He was 30 feet south, about to give it to another competitor! Ivan Steber, another BK who'd matched me on the swim, is one of the faster amps on the triathlon scene.

The bike section's steep hills tested me further before the 10k run's heat baked me. Dad witnessed my seemingly strong form at the 8k-point of the run where the majority of the spectators had gathered.

"You looked great!" he told me after the race.

"I was only looking strong for the sake of the crowd," I replied. The truth was, I was really suffering at that point. The final 5k had me walking a lot in the heat. I picked it up when I saw Dad, and even managed to catch a fellow competitor in a sprint to the finish line. The heat caused problems with Ivan's leg, and, battling blisters, he came in about 20 minutes behind me.

A few days later I traveled to Hawaii with a strong intention to break 11 hours at Ironman. Dad and Lillian joined me there.

I walked around Kona during the pre-race week with SUB 11 shaved into the back of my head. I figured this would be good psyche stuff. Throughout race week comments on the 'do came from all directions—mostly from behind. It gave me more reason to reach my goal.

I came out of the water 51 seconds ahead of my predicted swim time of one hour, 10 minutes. My bike time was 20 minutes faster than the year before with some credit due to Mother Nature for relaxing a bit on the crosswinds and headwinds on the way out to Hawi. Unfortunately, the unpleasant wind showed up on the ride back. I hopped off my bike exactly seven hours into the race. This left me with four hours to run the marathon, a split I felt I could hit on a perfect day.

But it wasn't a perfect day. By Mile 8, I had accepted the fact that I would come up short of my goal and devised an improvisational Plan B. At that point, I gave myself a goal of sub-11:30.

As I had the previous year, I stopped at several aid stations along the way to "chill out" Stumpie with ice water. The first stop caused a cramp in the left side of my groin and such tremendous pain that I was actually screaming in agony. A fellow competitor witnessed the problem as a volunteer was helping me walk it off. He offered me electrolyte pills to alleviate what was most likely a low-electrolyte-initiated muscle cramp. I took them; thankfully, the problem subsided and didn't return. (I still give thanks to that anonymous racer for his part in my successful day.)

One other problem occurred during the run: fatigue. Somewhere around Mile 14 I told myself that I would not subject myself to this misery again. I was weak and sore and not the least bit happy about it.

Despite the hours and miles I had dedicated to this year's race, I wasn't going much faster or feeling much stronger than I had the year before. I thought for a few minutes about how asinine an undertaking this was. I cursed myself for this ego-stroking display of drive and ability to tackle the Ironman—twice. *There's no way I'm coming back here again. Why am I doing this?*

The answer I needed came a couple of miles later.

The day before the race, I had set up an impromptu presentation at a middle school in the nearby town of Captain Cook. For whatever reason, the talk itself was mumbled and disconnected. Nevertheless, I must have left some type of good impression on the students. They had volunteered at the Mile 16 aid station, so I'd asked them to keep an eye out for me and provide a dose of energy. The kids went a step further.

As I approached the aid station, one of them yelled, "Here he comes!" The kids scrambled around and hoisted several banners, one of which read, "Go Stumpie!" The boys and girls went crazy as I ran by and I couldn't help feeling good again.

This time, as I approached the finish line, I took my own sweet time running down Ali'i Drive. I absorbed the crowd's energy, just soaked it up. I smiled and shed a couple of well-earned tears. I crossed the finish line with a time of 11:22:49, fast enough for happiness.

To top it off, at the finish line stood my father, with a big grin and open arms. What a great way to finish a race. I wish Mom could have been there too.

From Kona, I traveled to Maui for another first. This time it was not only a first for me, but an actual first, as in "the first person to…"

The XTERRA World Championships are held in Wailea, Maui each year. This off-road triathlon series was only four years old, so I was in prime position to be the first challenged individual to complete The Double: Ironman Hawaii then XTERRA eight days later.

Two months after the race, ESPN would broadcast the event and include a studio interview featuring me and footage of my struggling trail run—I was nowhere near recovered from the last weekend's Ironman. The race organizers were so impressed that they surprised me with a set of Spinergy SPOX mountain bike wheels at the awards ceremony.

The timing couldn't have been better. En route to Boulder from Hawaii, I returned to San Diego for my fourth consecutive San Diego Triathlon Challenge. That night the 180,000-mile engine in my '85 Civic Wagon said, "buh-bye." I sold my new bike wheels, used the cash to help finance a used motor from the local junkyard and was on my way home a few days later.

I spoke at three schools during the first week back in Colorado. Four races in five weeks on the road had given me more stories to share with students, who continually reminded me that I was helping to make a difference in their lives.

The Rebirth Berth

By this time it was clear that if I was going to make a Paralympic team, cycling would be the sport. I felt the pull: I would do whatever it took to be in Sydney the following October. I'd direct all my energies to making the team, set aside my love for triathlon to focus on the bike and be much better than I was now.

After the Ironman I rested for the entire month of November, except for my half-hearted participation in the 1999 San Diego Challenge, which is more of an event than a race. I looked forward to that weekend every year.

Kenny Souza, former and multiple Duathlon World Champion (run-bike-run), was my relay team runner. He left the transition before I even finished the ride. The 58-miler took me no less than four-and-a-half hours. Pooped from both Kona and Maui, I chose to take it easy and enjoy the ride.

I warned a few friends that I might take awhile, but they scoffed at any suggestion that I could actually relax on race day. To prove them all wrong, I lounged around on various inviting pieces of real estate along the course while waiting for, among others, one-legged friends Shawn Brown (discus), Tom Bourgeois (pentathlon) and Matt Perkins (alpine skiing) to catch up.

I'd made it only a few miles past my final resting spot when I found myself helping a fellow participant with a flat tire, then helping him again when he flatted a second time. Back at transition, the PA announcer declared to the crowd, "We don't know what happened to two-time national cycling champion Paul Martin; he's been out there for over four hours!"

The SDTC was the only activity that raised my heart rate over 120 beats per minute before December, when Coach Kathy put me on a program that included significant time spent in the gym.

When I started training again on December 1, I logged a combination of miles on the stationary trainer, on the rollers and on the road. I even did a few spin classes. My single leg press max reached 450 pounds by March—on the prosthetic side. I cycled a total of 3,300 miles and spent nearly 60 hours weight training before the late April Paralympic Track Trials, which were held in Frisco, Texas, 20 miles outside of Dallas. The state-of-the-art outdoor 250-meter track simulated the indoor track to be used in Sydney. Both velodromes have 44-degree banked turns that require a minimum speed of 16 m.p.h. to prevent sliding down the track, removing skin.

My experience entering the season's first race was from earlier in April, when I spent two days on the Alecdrome in Houston and on the Superdrome in Frisco. The flu had wiped me out for six days leading up to this introductory track training. I made my debut as a track racer the day after I arrived in Houston, without having sat on a bike in a week, with the bug still in me. The mass-start races (multiple riders on the track at once) got easier as the night progressed, but I thought I was going to pass out after the first few sprints.

On the final day of training in Frisco, track coach Ryan Crissey told me to ride the four-kilometer pursuit at full effort. I clocked a time of five minutes, 46 seconds. It was a windy day, I was riding a rented, spoke-wheeled bike and I was both sick and tired. I knew I could have ridden a 5:20 on a good day.

I still didn't have a track bike or decent wheels. I was forced to borrow race wheels from a friend in Boulder for the Paralympic trials in Texas two weeks later back at the Superdrome. The borrowed wheels were a carbon fiber rear disk and a three-spoke carbon front wheel. Despite the designed-for-airline-travel hard shell wheel transporter, which I carefully packed them in, the airline crew managed to totally destroy both wheels. They arrived in Texas looking as if the jet itself had run them over.

The wheels may have been crushed, but my spirit remained intact. I had spoken in nearly two dozen schools in the previous four months and my major theme remained, as Virginia Woolf once wrote, to "arrange whatever pieces come your way."

And "pieces" did come my way. The neutral support mechanic loaned me a rear disc and a yet-to-be-released prototype spoked front wheel.

Perhaps the most exciting part of the event preceded the race itself. For four or five minutes just before the gun went off, I reminded myself over and over and over again that I had committed myself, that I had subjected myself to unwelcome miles and hours on the bike for one reason—to go to Sydney—and no one was going to take that away from me.

I lined up against my good friend Ron Williams, who'd been training under the tutelage of Chris Carmichael, Lance Armstrong's personal coach. A month before trials, Ron had topped my efforts on the power meter at the Olympic Training Center's physiology lab, and he had been matching me on our road rides. On a group training ride that week in Colorado Springs, consisting mostly of Cat Ones and Twos, Ron and I stayed near the front of the pack for the entire ride. We were both committed to racing in Sydney.

At 26 years of age, Ron knew he could be a faster rider and he knew he needed to be in order to win medals in Sydney. But that would require a total commitment to the 2000 Paralympic Games. In June, Ron's employer granted him a paid leave of absence to spend time at the Olympic Training Center in Colorado Springs, to become the best he could be.

The Paralympic cycling team would consist of 25 athletes (15 qualified on the track and 10 on the road) from three separate disabilities: amputee, blind and cerebral palsy. Of the 21 athletes who raced the track trials in Frisco, the top 15 riders whose times came closest to their particular disability's world record qualified for the team.

I raced my ass off in the 4k pursuit and qualified for the Paralympic team with a time of 5:17. Ron finished in 5:22 and likewise earned a spot. He was quite happy to have nearly solidified an invitation to Sydney; he was not happy that his time was five seconds slower than mine.

My effort put me in third place overall, right behind Dory Selinger.

Ron was sixth. The mixed tandem team of blind rider Pam Fernandez and her pilot Al Whaley took first.

Finally. *Finally.* I had a Paralympic Team berth. Three sports later.

…Finally.

I raced in a few big cycling events around the country in the spring and summer of 2000: New Mexico's Tour of the Gila in May, the Fitchburg Longsjo Classic over the Fourth of July weekend near my hometown and the National Disabled Cycling Championships among the corn fields of Indiana. My performances at nationals were less than stellar, and bronze in the road race was my only placing. But I did what I had to do to make the road team in Sydney: eliminate Gary Sehgi.

My place in the Sydney race was decided: I would be the *domestique*, the guy who does all the work so someone else can win the race. Fine with me. Work is good. It builds character. I was feeling *so* ready for Sydney.

Through August, I had considered the track races in Sydney as participatory. My qualifying times in Frisco were well out of medal contention. But at the training camp in Colorado Springs six weeks before the Paralympics, I posted times in both the 4k pursuit and kilo that would have put me in the medals at the '98 World Championships. All of a sudden I had a whole new outlook toward the Games. *Medals galore!*

Being ready to race was obviously important, but what I tried hard to focus on was truly experiencing the training for my first Paralympic event. The race itself would be such a small part of that experience. What really matters, I decided, is absorbing the richness of the process that gets you there.

Sydney

I'm an athlete—a cyclist and, primarily, a triathlete. Pretty basic stuff. Lots of people race bikes and do triathlons. I find it hard to believe that riding a bike makes me much of a celebrity, but apparently it does.

I rode through Sydney Olympic Park on a beautiful Saturday afternoon in October, 2000. I wore my Team USA jersey and shorts for an easy spin session all by my lonesome. I wondered at the magnificent architecture of Sydney Stadium, the Superdome and the Aquatic Center. In the midst of this pleasant experience a young boy stopped me with a question.

"May I have your autograph?"

"Uh…sure."

Then an elderly lady in a flowered scarf pulled out her Paralympic program and asked me to sign the inside cover. Then a Korean couple in their 50s did the same, followed by a few bright-eyed Aussie kids. Then a little girl approached me for a photo without saying a word, almost too shy to do so; her father was ready with the camera. I picked her up, put her on my handlebars and together we smiled.

"Thank you very much," they said in unison before she ran back into his arms.

"You are *very* welcome," I said.

Three young Japanese women came up to me, smiling. "May we take photo?" one asked as the other two flanked me and my Schwinn.

"Of course." How could I refuse?

One woman clicked and all three giggled. They were so excited to pose with a random American cyclist who had yet to win a medal. Then the rotation began. The picture-taker moved over to the spot vacated by the young woman on my left, who had moved to my right, and the original one on the right was now lining us up for another shot, and so on. Finally, they all did the Japanese bow-in-respect thing, giggled some more, and watched me mount the bike and slowly ride away, laughing to myself. *I'm just a cyclist.*

This is how I felt much of the time in Australia: like unworthy royalty. The staff at the Paralympic Village (same as the Olympic Village, two weeks later) did our laundry, changed our sheets, provided unlimited food 24/7 and smiled every time we walked by. I kept thinking, *What did I ever do to deserve being treated so well?*

I train and race because I like to. Not because I have to. In doing this thing that I love, in living this lifestyle that I enjoy so much, I've become one of the better prosthetic-wearing riders in the world. Fourth fastest kilometer track racer in the world, if you were to go by Paralympic cycling's opening race at the indoor Dunc Gray Velodrome earlier in the week.

As a reward for being a dedicated athlete, the U.S. Olympic Committee invested thousands of dollars in me for a flight to Australia and to house me in the Paralympic Village. They provided a modest amount of national attention. The Xerox Corporation, a USOC sponsor, produced a magazine-style, 50-odd page publication titled *Chasing the Olympic Dream* that featured dozens of events and only six individuals. I was one of the six and the only highlighted cyclist, able-bodied or not. The two-page layout penned me as "one of America's best hopes for a medal." *USA Today* dedicated the entire back page to me in their June 3, 1999 paper. It was part of their *Olympic Glory* monthly feature section with several full-color photos.

I had lost my leg in a car accident, tried to prove to myself that I was still "able," and eight years later the country's most widely read newspaper showcased me as an upcoming Olympian. *Unbelievable.*

My father was there to witness my efforts against the best competition the world had to offer. I could hear his deep, overachieving cheers on every single lap. He was proud of me—he'd told me so. The night before the road race he told me that I'd achieved so much more than he had ever even thought of by the time he was my age: 33 years. He expressed his sincere appreciation for my ambition. That meant so much to me, particularly because of our once tumultuous relationship…after the years of wishing he would never come home from work.

Things had changed. That was almost 20 years ago. Now Dad had traveled to the other side of the world to sit in the stands, hoping I might win a medal representing my country in the most prestigious of all athletic events. After all, I told everybody I would; I was confident I'd bring back some hardware. I didn't *promise* anyone I'd win a medal, but I did say this to hundreds of supporters: *I can guarantee you one thing—I'll ride my ass off!*

On Day One of the Games at the Velodrome, I was getting ready to race my first international kilo. The race official, along with U.S. track coaches Tim Roach and Ryan Crissey, positioned my bike in the starting gate. I straddled the bike carefully, deliberately. As soon as my cleats were clicked into the pedals, the clock began ticking down from 30 seconds. I took my hands off the bars to relax my upper body. I took a few deep belly breaths, smiled and thought: *Look at me. On the line at the Olympics. How lucky am I?*

I glanced across the track and saw my father smiling too. I gave him a little finger-point confirmation. Then I looked up, in the midst of the emotion, to thank my Maker for putting me there. The honor of being on this line sporting the Stars & Stripes choked me up a bit. I was getting ready to bust out of the gate and do what I'd been trained to do. Like a Marine jumping off the boat at Normandy. OK, not quite that nerve-racking.

Four racers had gone before me. One of them was my good friend Ron Williams. He expected a much faster time than the 1:15:51 he posted. I was bummed that he didn't ride a record-breaker, happy he'd left the window open. I knew I could beat his time.

At 10 seconds to go the clock beeped. I thanked Him again. My hands were back on the bars and my fanny found its position. Five seconds. The beeper then beeped away each second on the big numeric counter in front of me. With one second to go, I meticulously slid an inch backward on the saddle, ready to lunge. The simulated gunfire sounded and I exploded out of the hydraulic starting gate. Arms locked, hips forward, head up and breathing deeply. *Go! Go! Go!*

It's all about power. The efficient transfer from total body to the pedals. Pulling up and pushing down—simultaneously. I pushed a big gear: 94 inches. That's how far the bike traveled with one complete 360-degree pedal rotation. My gearing was probably the largest of all in my category, maybe even bigger than the one-arm dudes. I wasn't much of a spinner—a rider comfortable at a high rpm—so I went for the big masher ratio of 49x14. That's 49 teeth in the front chain ring and 14 teeth on the rear cog. This made for a slow start and I had one of the slowest opening laps—23.1 seconds—on the 250-meter track. For the less mathematical, the kilo is a four-lap race.

Of the 13 international starters, my second lap was the second fastest; once you get that big gear rolling, it rolls. By the start of the third lap, the lactate in my legs was markedly building up and my breathing was becoming labored. By the end of the third lap, I had next to nothing left in the tank; that's how you're supposed to ride a kilo. In turn two of the last lap, I took the advice of team mechanic Mark Legg: "Picture the stiffest competition trying to come around you. Then turn on the jets and shut him down." I emptied the tank—left it all on the track—and crossed the line in 1:14:88. First place…for a little while.

Like Ron's performance, my time was a bit disappointing. I had fantasized about breaking the world record of 1:10.6.

Six riders down, seven to go. I had to rely on the remaining competition to have substandard rides, not such a great position to be in. The next three posted slower times and I held onto the top spot. There were four riders left and only three medals to win. Czech star Jiri Jezek posted a 1:15 at the World Championships a couple of years ago. He was rider #11 and clocked an astonishing 1:11:46. *Suck it up Paul. He's got experience. This is your second kilo…ever.* (The first was at the Paralympic trials in Frisco, Texas, six months earlier.)

There were three riders left. The order: Australian Paul Lake, Frenchman Patrice Ceria, then American Dory Selinger—the world record holder. Patrice Ceria was a weak kilo rider. I knew that. Paul had been focusing on the four-kilometer pursuit race that would be held a few days later. Rumor had had it he wasn't even going to ride the kilo. He rode slower than me through the first two laps of his kilo. *Holy shit*, I said to myself from my trackside cool-down stationary trainer, *Ceria's no trackie…Holy shit, I might get a medal!* On the third lap Paul held his speed and had me by a tenth of a second. When he crossed the finish line I was in third place with two riders to go. *Shit.*

The Frenchman rode next with an expectedly slower time of 1:16. Then came Dory, the world record holder. Short of some type of catastrophe, which I wouldn't wish on any competitor, my medal was about to dance into the arms of another.

Dory rode a 1:11:81 for the silver medal. The gold went to Jiri—his first ever in international competition. No one deserved it more.

At first I was a little bent, but I soon found myself content with my fourth place finish. Those who beat me out of the medals were all much more experienced than I was. It wouldn't be reasonable to expect everything to go my way at my first Paralympics. I was more of an aerobic guy anyway. The 4k pursuit was in a couple of days and that was my kinda race: drawn out a bit.

Two days later, Ron and Australia's Daniel Polson were first up to race the pursuit, each starting together at the midpoint of the straightaway on opposite sides of the track. Neither posted significantly impressive times: 5:13:29 and 5:10:60, respectively. Ron was bummed again. I didn't blame him.

As expected, the next two riders did no damage. I was scheduled to ride with a Brazilian but for some technical reason, he had to forfeit from the race, as he had done for the kilo. I would ride solo. The crowd was all mine.

Coach Crissey ordered me to hold steady at 19.0 seconds per lap. If I went any harder, he said he'd knock me off the track himself. Ron had gone too hard in his race and had run out of juice early. Hence, his slow time and my coach's warning. Coach Crissey barked out my splits as I came by his corner on each lap. I was right on target for the first thirteen laps: 18.8s to 19.2s. Then I kicked it for the final 750 meters with lap times of 19.1, 19.2, 18.8. A "technically perfect" race according to Coach Roach. Those splits were designed to edge out Daniel Polson.

But I came up less than a second short of Polson's time. I posted a 5:11:48. *Damn it!*

At first I was seriously pissed at Coach Crissey for assigning splits that put me directly into second. I mean, that's the advantage of being seeded higher; you know what needs to be done. In the end, I learned that I was supposed to have gone a little faster on my opening lap and a little faster in the last three. That was the difference. Besides that, the big guns—Jiri, Paul, and Dory—all followed. Jiri's incredible effort posted a new world record time of 4:59:67, then he broke that one in the finals with a time of 4:58:52. Paul rode a 5:00:64. Then Dory rode a 5:04. Those three would have schooled me in the energy-draining finals anyway and a medal would have been an unresolved pipe dream.

OK. The road race was in a few days and I'd be plenty rested. *I'm a roadie.*

For months I had focused primarily on the road race. It would come down to a sprint, if I didn't work to make it otherwise. I was not a sprinter—and I knew next to nothing about tactics. Truthfully, I am a triathlete, a hammerhead who is good at putting my head down for long, hard miles without a lot of fluctuation in effort. My job in Sydney was to wear down the competition, to take the legs out of 'em, leave them nothing left for the sprint to the line, and have one of my teammates take the win. That was the plan. As it turned out, I had to do everything I could just to hang on to the other riders.

The race, held in Sydney's Centennial Park, was 63.9 kilometers, short for a road race. Sixty-three point nine miles would have been more typical. But the relatively short race packed a whole lotta pain. That harmless bump of a hill midway through the course worked me. It worked my teammate Ron, too. On the fifth of seven laps, we lost contact with the pack halfway up the hill—and we're both good climbers. The others were better.

Europeans dominate the cycling world—with the exception, of course, of Lance Armstrong. Me? I'm a triathlete doing my best to be a roadie for the sake of this very race. *Get back on.*

The race pushed my limits from the start. Jiri attacked at the base of the hill. I chased and the others followed. That little hill hurt so much. It was only about 800 meters long at a six- or seven-percent grade, *but it hurt.* The next few laps mirrored the first; either Jiri, one of the Frenchmen or I attacked on the hill. By the fifth lap, the hill damn near knocked me out of the race.

The hard, nearly 180-degree left-hander at the top of the hill was 30 seconds away and the pack was almost there already. Ron and I were off the back, out of immediate contact with the peloton and we swapped pulls to reach the top before they got too far away. We reached the top, exhausted, but could not let up. We had to get back on. It wasn't looking good for the Americans at this point; we had lost Dory a couple laps ago.

Gotta get back on. This is what I do—I race. Get back on. I got up front and Ron got on my wheel—into my slipstream or draft zone. He was hurting, bad. That solo lap #3 he did off the front of the pack reminded him of what it means to be patient, to save the juice for later. (Riding solo uses up approximately 30 percent more energy than riding with the momentum of others.)

I pulled; that is to say, I led the pack, breaking the ambient air and making it 30 percent easier for those who followed—Ron and one of the Frenchies who had two of his teammates in the break. He wasn't going to do any work; he wasn't going to help us catch his teammates. Ron recovered and pulled for a few pedal strokes to give me a chance to breathe. Then I did what I do best. "Get on Ron, I'm putting the hammer down." I'd hammer for a mile or so, then I'd refuel behind Ron for a few pedal strokes. Again, I'd get back at the front.

I heard my father cheering for me each round as we passed the start/finish line. He told me he'd pray for me. God, how he'd changed. I'd become quite proud of him.

"The Americans are 20 seconds back," the announcer told the Sydneysider crowd, "and the pack's looking strong." *Look all you want. I'm stronger.* A half mile later, foaming at the mouth, I was back on with Ron and the French guy in tow.

We raced by the congregations of school children from all over New South Wales who had been brought in by the state to witness something spectacular: the Paralympic Games. Four thousand individuals with more than your average challenge, rising to the occasion. Those kids were so incredibly LOUD. Little people screaming "Go Aussie! Go Aussie!" How they do love sport down there.

Then we hit the hill again. Unfortunately, Ron missed the boat this time. The pack, with me in it, made the big turn at the top. I looked over to see Ron crawling up the hill with his head down. Poor guy. This race meant so much to him. I'd already beaten him by one spot in the kilo and by one spot in the pursuit. Ron was a great friend, but he was also the competition when you got down to it. He wanted to be on top today. Ron was off the back.

The peloton was timid for a stretch. No one wanted to pull into the wind—let the other guys do the work. I wasn't volunteering—both of my teammates were out. The Frenchies were three. The Aussies and the Germans each had two. I was by myself. So was arguably the world's best prosthetic-wearing cyclist, Czech Republican Jiri Jezek.

Meanwhile, Ron emptied his tank. He's no quitter. "I'm back on," I heard him say.

"Nice!"

Then the pace picked up.

One lap to go. As we neared the feed zone, I felt a leg cramp developing in the good leg, in both my hamstring and calf. I opted to reach for a bottle of de-fizzed cola, which provides sugar, electrolytes and water. Then Jiri attacked.

Forced to bypass the drink and having slowed up a hair to get it, I had to get out of the saddle at 100 percent to keep from getting dropped again. That's when the cramps hit full force. I was back on but I didn't think I could hold on with the pain consuming my entire right leg. Luckily, the pace let up enough for me to reach down, administer a bit of self-massage, and help alleviate the problem. The pain subsided, then the pace picked up.

Jiri, despite his two-lap solo effort, kept attacking. He was like that. He was like that the year before in France at the European Championships. He was like that the year before that at the World Championships in Colorado Springs.

On our final climb up the big little hill, Patrice Ceria, the reigning Paralympic Champion, turned up the heat. *Shit!* With my heart rate pegged, I was off the back—again. A good 30 meters off the back. That was it—the last climb had dropped me.

Bullshit! Empty the fucking tank!

I got out of the saddle and gave it everything my one and a half legs could give. *Empty the fucking tank! This is the Paralympics for crissakes. You're not here to almost stay with them. You are them. They need to get rid of you. Those repeat hill climbs in Boulder were meant for this moment. Those lactate threshold-building power climbs were made for this shit. You're a full-timer to be the best you can be, better than the rest. You leave anything on this hill and when you're 80 you'll be wishing you would've tried just a little harder. Empty the tank!*

I emptied it and got back on. All of a sudden I was mentally juiced. *I'm one of the best. No one drops me!* They can try, but trust me, it's not that easy. I reached the top with the rest of them, turned the corner, and then looked around for Ron. He was waaaay back there, head down, crawlin'. Game over this time.

Four kilometers to go; same deal, no one wanted to pull. As we all looked at each other, I heard Ron. "I'm back on," he said.

"Nice! Nice! Nice!"

Ron is pure guts. It was guts that got him through the bone cancer that claimed his left foot at the age of 14. It was guts that got him four overall world championship titles in water skiing with three standing world records. It was guts that got him to Sydney.

There was one kilo to go.

Of all the Paralympic categories, we, the BK amputees riding with a prosthetic, had the deepest talent pool. Nearly everyone in our group had a shot at winning the road race. Only a few of the original 14 starters were not in the finish line pack. The lone Brazilian, the squirrelly rider, got dropped early in the race. As for the English chap, we knew he'd be off before long. And Dory had pulled out of the race after his third lap. He liked his pain in short, high intensity doses. He was a trackie.

I sat third in the pace line as we passed under the "one kilometer" banner. The pace was conservative. Everyone was saving it for the sprint to the finish line.

Seven hundred meters to go.

We rode by the team tent, where the U.S. delegation was cheering for Ron and me. I was still about third, riding on the right, exactly where I wanted to be, using the others to shield the left side wind. This was one of very few bike races I'd ever ridden wisely—I was usually the guy pulling everyone around the course. Riding smart was why I sat third in the pack. That's why I had plenty left in the tank—despite that big little hill.

Boom! Daniel Polson jumped and the sprint began to wind up. *OK. Here we go.* A week and a half ago I showed the world that I was the fourth fastest kilo rider on the planet. The third fastest was somewhere behind me right now. The second fastest had dropped out of the race already. And the fastest fastest was on my left, taking some of the wind.

It was my race to win.

The pace was 90 percent. The finish line was 200 meters away. In about two seconds I was going to have to let it all hang out...

Jiri wasn't giving me much room. There was about a five-foot gap between him on my left and the temporary steel barriers on my right. That was fine; I didn't need much room. A bike width, that's all. And I had it.

Daniel, the Aussie, was half a bike length in front of Jiri, who was half a bike length in front of me. As far as I could tell, I was still sitting third.

Perfect. Suddenly, in an effort to throw wind into the face of his chasers, Daniel made a quick move to his right—oh, how I wish he would have gone left. The move pushed Jiri to his right, right into me. Since his wheel was lapping mine, and he was just a hair too far in front of me to get an elbow on him; I was forced to go right. I tried to keep from hitting the fence but my momentum was going that way and, at 35 miles an hour, I was riding over the 10-inch long, two-inch wide, quarter-inch thick barrier footings, which lessened my ability to stay upright.

Damn, I'm losing it! I'm going down!... Fuck that! With a quick throw of the bike to the outside, my knuckles rattled against the barriers, removing skin, but I stayed up. Bloody knuckles and all. Regretfully, in the process my prosthetic side unclipped from the pedal. *Shit! Shit! Shit!!!*

Click.

Miraculously, what normally takes full attention and a smidgen of time, at the very least, happened instantly: I was back in my pedal! *Go! Go! Go! Get it back! Get it back!*

Nope...

Sorry...

It doesn't work that way.

Momentum is everything in a finish line sprint and I had just lost mine. In those two or three missed pedal strokes, four riders got ahead of me. The game was over. Seventh place. No Paralympic medals for me.

I was bummed out...for about 30 seconds. Then I congratulated myself for riding one hell of a good race.

The Rolling Stones told us, sometime in the late '60s, "You can't always get what you want/But if you try sometime you just might find/You get what you need." Short of dying from starvation, this statement is ultimately precise. You *always* get what you need. I wanted to win a gold medal. I had three shots at the prize and, well, a bronze medal would have tickled me pink. It wasn't in the cards.

No biggie, I'll get mine. I'd gotten mine already, really. I was there. I was above ground. I was a Paralympian. I could ride a bike *really* fast. I'd been blessed.

I only have five toes, but I have been blessed.

Afterthoughts

This book contains my thoughts, experiences, beliefs, and opinions. I don't profess to be a great philosopher. All I know about philosophy is its definition, which I had to look up in my copy of *Webster's 9th Collegiate Dictionary* (which states that philosophy is, "the most general beliefs, concepts and attitudes of an individual or group").

I don't much care to debate my beliefs or opinions, as I see no point in trying to convince people to see things my way. I'll gladly offer you my thoughts and feelings, but rarely do I feel with conviction that my way is the right way. We all see the world through a unique set of eyes: our own. What motivates us is possibly the greatest distinction between individuals: different desires, passions and purposes.

By putting my thoughts on paper I've come to a better understanding of myself. I have written about attitudes which, if held, might enable some people to see things in a brighter light. I haven't taken these positions myself at every opportunity, but as someone once told me, "The best way to learn something is to teach it." While teaching was not my main motivation for writing this book, baring my beliefs for the sake of setting my own higher standard was a part of it. Having laid down my convictions, I'm creating a person I hope to emulate. To live up to my own standards would surely bring resolve. It would reduce what distress I do own.

Naturally, introspection became a part of the process. I wrote about shameful experiences (some of which I took out of the manuscript) and by doing so have purged my system to some degree. As any good therapist will tell you, his or her job is to listen. In this work I have had to listen to myself over and over again. On occasion, I hoped to clarify my feelings by writing about them, then realized that's not how I felt at all. I had never before taken the time to look at some things, and when I did, I found false assumptions within myself. In effect, I have made you, the reader, my listener and now have little to hide.

In grasping my own feelings, I'm in a better position to help others with theirs. You may have heard the phrase, "Never trust a fat doctor." If I hope to be there for others, it's best to be there for myself first.

Some of my motivation to write came from a concern for the future. I believe it is important to rear our children in such a way as to promote love, caring and intelligent choices. While this book is no manual for parenting, I feel the attitude we show while raising children is half the battle. If we intend to solve such major problems in the world as war, poverty and discrimination, we need to set examples of how to do so. Children learn hate from others. They learn love from others too. Let's make that a priority. I'm not schooled in the field of education, but I do not need to be shown which generalities are good and which are not.

I write simply. I don't expect you, the reader, to be awed by my use of the English language. If it weren't for my friends, the editors, you would be less impressed still. I had an interesting story to tell and in that telling, I was granted an avenue to communicate my beliefs. I would like to think that this work might inspire some of you to begin chasing your dreams. Or to view the world's developments a little more lightheartedly. Or to take up triathlon.

I give thanks for all the experiences I've had in my life so far. *All* of them. They've provided me with a better understanding of my greater purpose for having been put here in the first place. Like Dad used to say: "No one ever said it was going to be easy."

I am especially grateful for the joys with which I have been blessed. I have learned that I possess athletic ability. Jason Lalla, Paralympic gold medallist in alpine skiing, honored me with a dubious distinction: he once told me that I was one of the best athletes he'd ever known, because I had accomplished national team membership in four different sports. Genes deserve a great deal of credit, but the hours and miles of training deserve the most. (And I'm really not the best athlete he's ever known; that's just not possible.)

It really comes down to commitment. The dedication it takes to prepare for an event like the Ironman involves more than time and physical "doing." Like most worthwhile and consuming undertakings, it takes a commitment of the heart, which anybody can possess if they have a passion for reaching the finish line.

Jim MacLaren gets partial credit for my experiences. He currently holds the BK marathon record of three hours and 15 minutes and also the Hawaiian Ironman record with a time of 10 hours, 38 minutes. Rivaldo Martins broke the overall Ironman distance record in the year 2000 in 10 hours, 31 minutes at Ironman Europe, in Germany. (Hawaii's conditions are tougher.) Jim gave me the inspiration to take up the sport of triathlon. Like so many other first-timers, I became hooked.

Bill Bell earned the honor of "world's oldest Ironman," covering the distance within the allotted 17 hours, at age 76. Judy Molnar crossed the finish line of the Hawaiian Ironman, as well. Her six-foot, one-inch frame lost 120 pounds after her doctor termed her "morbidly obese."

I choose to direct my energy and focus toward the various disciplines I pursue. Money, relationships and career have all been put on the back burner. I truly feel that I have been blessed with more than pure ability or talent; what makes my goals possible is persistence and dedication, and a philosophy described this way by Robert C. Savage: "You can measure a man by the adversity it takes to discourage him."

My life experiences have taught me that the setbacks are often gifts— opportunities to do it better the next time.

Many of the hardships of ironworking came in handy as an amputee; similarities exist between the two. To begin with, there's the hardware. Ironworkers and amputees alike need the tools: an ironworker needs a hammer, spud wrenches, and a butt-load of bolts; an amputee needs a leg, a liner, and a butt-load of stump socks. Look a bit deeper and you'll see they both need courage, acceptance of physical pain, and an ability to deal with the weather. Distance running on a hot, humid day is a recipe for an abrasion blister on a less-than-perfect-fitting socket.

My experiences with my father have affected me in a way that will surely benefit my own family someday. My understanding of him as a man and his love for me has come full circle. Just as I know I have always loved him, despite the teenage years when I wished he were dead, I now know he always loved me—he simply had trouble revealing his feelings, and I had trouble asking for anything.

The loss of loved ones has taught me that life can, and will, go on. But a little piece of those you've loved stays with you. I believe that they went to a better place and that they *just might* be back among us somehow, someday.

My broken romances have taught me much about myself, about what is really important to me. During this process, I have learned that certain moments spent with the woman you love are about as close to Heaven on Earth as it gets.

The loss of my leg has taught me that I am not contained within my body. My body merely does what I ask of it, at least for the time being. I have been able to use my body as a tool, a vehicle through which I have learned a great deal about the human spirit. The international athletic competition I enjoy has helped me look beyond the expected and get the most out of each day that I am given. That's not to say that I actually do, but I try.

Until December 12, 1992, I absolutely expected to keep all of my limbs throughout my life. I discovered, traumatically, that any part of my body can be quickly taken away. I had taken my health for granted, but, as a result of the accident, I was forced to take a closer look at everything I took for granted, including the future and my personal potential.

My path led to an opportunity to represent my country in athletics. When I reflect back honestly, I realize that I had the opportunity twice. The first time, with two legs, I overlooked my abilities and didn't reach my athletic potential. That's not necessarily a crime, but I did neglect to take advantage.

My friends are a major factor in my ability to remain on this ship of fortune that I have chosen to board. My reliance on friendships has shown me that help is there if you need it, something that has made my own ability to assist others that much more gratifying.

My mother is one of the most caring and wonderful people I have ever known.

I believe you cannot expect too much from anyone or anything. Strive and take what comes; it's a wonderful way to sidestep disappointment. Your happiness is not owed to you. Your happiness is self-fulfilling.

I have learned that religion and spirituality are two different things. The former is structured; the latter is a completely personal thing. I was raised Catholic and never believed much of what I was taught about Christianity. Things like believing in Noah's Ark and that "the world was created in seven days" were too shaky for me to take seriously. Doubt made it difficult for me to accept religion and I became an agnostic; I felt guilty going to church on Christmas day.

And yet, lying in the hospital after the accident that claimed my left foot, drenched in cold sweat in the middle of the night and unable to sleep, I found respite from the loneliness by praying to God. They were, admittedly, guilt-ridden prayers—desperate measures. It was hypocritical, I thought at the time, to turn to religion when I had ignored it on a regular basis. Now I realize I was turning toward spirituality, sincerely.

I never asked, "Why me?" It was my fault. What I begged for was that the pain would go away. I asked Him/Her/It to help me get through my ordeal. But I felt guilty doing so.

Recently I have lost all doubt about whether or not there is something wonderful that put me here. I can't explain just how I became open to this knowledge. It just happened. Partial credit goes to Cynthia Diane Ling. We met through triathlon in 1998. A deeply spiritual person, she asked at the time how I felt about these matters of the soul. I told her I didn't give much credence to the idea of a soul because there wasn't enough hard evidence. Cynthia said, "I think you're more spiritual than you realize."

Somehow, soon after that conversation, I started feeling differently about myself, as well as everyone and everything around me.

The best advice I have ever been given wasn't given to me at all. It came from within. I learned to trust my instincts—they rarely let me down. I also believe in being defined by the "Big Picture," the major viewpoints that characterize each of us. The choices I have made about the road I travel, the philosophies I explore and the people I befriend have been my own. True, along the way I have relied on mentors, both inside and outside of my family, to assist me. But I have defined the points that embody my character myself.

My mistakes have been my greatest teachers. Many of these teachers required me to repeat their lessons due to my lack of attention, faltering memory or good old-fashioned stubbornness. It's a rare occasion when I will not venture along a path for fear of making a mistake. Humiliation—yes. Peer pressure—yes. Physical pain—yes. But for fear of possibly screwing it up—no. Has this attitude ever gotten me into trouble? Oh, yeah. But, it works for me. I would rather make a mistake than make an excuse.

In the past 10 years, I have learned to be myself and not worry about how others present themselves or judge my behavior. I'm also getting better at working on myself instead of criticizing others, but I still have some refining to do. Dr. Wayne Dyer described it this way: "One way to have the tallest building in town is to tear down all the others. The second way to have the tallest building in town is to work on your own, ignoring the height of the other buildings."

I'm putting an addition on my own building by writing this book. Like it or not, this is how I feel. This is me, naked and honest.

Maintaining this attitude, and being able to express it, is a change I've gone through in my life. The transformation was not an overnight occurrence. It was, and still is, an integral part of my human and spiritual development: part of my evolution. With each passing day I'm learning to accept myself and appreciate myself. I'm learning to value diversity in others as well as in myself.

I must admit, I still find myself judging others. Most frequently I judge those whose characteristics resemble mine of days both past and present, and possibly future. The slacker teenager, the boasting playboy, the yuppie, the struggling artist, the ski bum. I still "judge" them, but I no longer condemn them. I find myself subconsciously assessing their decisions but I have no opinion of their effect. I see people doing harmless things that I would consider bad choices—quitting high school for example, or tattooing their faces. But by virtue of their desire to walk a particular path and learn from it or to simply enjoy it for what it is, their choice is often the right one.

Oddly enough, I judge criminals, even though I've driven drunk, shoplifted and have lied on my tax return. Who am I to rate their actions? This is something I struggle with.

People sometimes justify their actions by claiming that if another person did it, it should be fine that they do the same. If anything, that's all the more reason not to. Littering is a good example. The problem is obvious. The more people litter, the more environmental degradation takes place. Let's look at a more pertinent example: vindictiveness. If individuals, factions or even nations look to settle the score by striking back for some action they feel has wronged them, the end result will be more conflict. There is no advancement contained within vindictive behavior.

This is no great insight, but I suggest compassion, empathy and forgiveness as an alternative.

I sometimes justify my own questionable thoughts and actions with the position that I haven't brought harm to others. Is that the only yardstick for determining whether an act is right or wrong? That sounds like a partial definition of justice to me. Maybe someone suffered and nobody knew about it. Maybe I suffered and didn't take the time to notice. Bringing harm to oneself cannot be considered acceptable either.

By no means do I pretend to be an example of proper behavior. I still say "fuck" more than most people. I still drive like an asshole. I enjoy a cold beer or a Jack & Coke. I humbly remain myself.

I have reached a level of peace with myself. My days are not filled with regrets and distress. The choices I have made, at least the more recent ones, reflect my intentions. My development toward a more spiritual philosophy has made these choices, toward personal fulfillment through athletics instead of financial and corporate success, less questionable. They were right simply because I honestly felt they were.

The question will undoubtedly recur, "How long do you see yourself doing this, Paul?" My answer will most likely be, "Until I find something else I'd rather be doing." I think that covers it quite well. Maybe I'll be able to make a comfortable living speaking to kids. Maybe I'll begin to address corporations. At the moment, I can't imagine working nine to five for a company (or should I say eight to six?), but I'm not ruling it out. I might go back to school. I might become an actor. I could do that. I can see myself working in the public sector, perhaps in some type of political office. Who knows? Maybe I'll become a writer, although this book, my first work, might not sell outside my circle of friends. I have recently taken an interest in psychology and ecology, but right now they're just interests. I can say that I have this "gotta save the world" thing going on right now. We'll have to wait and see how long that lasts. I can certainly see myself being a triathlete for a long, long time. "He who knows not where he's going, goes the highest," states Cromwell.

I'm thankful that I have the capacity to learn these things, and in the process I've come to understand that I have so much more to learn that I'll never be finished with my "education." I also see that there is no need to understand everything. What I need to know I will learn. What baffles me is sometimes best left alone for the sake of economy and efficiency.

Pirsig stated in *Zen and The Art of Motorcycle Maintenance*, "Peace of mind produces right values, right values produce right thoughts. Right thoughts produce right actions and right actions produce work which will be a material reflection for others to see of the serenity at the center of it all." Peace of mind—that's where it's at. I believe it starts with love. Love of everyone and everything. Yes, it takes considerable effort—like most worthwhile things.

There is one last thing I have learned, perhaps the most important lesson so far. I have come to realize that no individual is too small to make a difference in the world. The difference might be small. Or big.

Why not big? We're all human. That's where all the great ones started.

I was told that I could make a difference in my own survival but I don't recall being told that, if I really wanted to, I could make a difference in the world. That's where a child learns that he or she has value as a person. That's when they learn that they're part of a bigger picture. When the responsibility is put on them, when they are challenged to have a positive effect on their surroundings, they will harness an inherently benign tendency to lend a hand and develop an understanding of their worth. There is a need for parents, teachers, and mentors to instill early in the development of a child's worldview that there is a better way for humankind to perpetuate itself. The way things are is not necessarily the way things should remain.

We are all in this together. It's not us against them. It's Us. This addresses the question, Where does our loyalty truly belong? Community, nation, world? I think the answer is a bit of each. Let's work together for improved communities, nations...and a better world.

The dream of global peace does not have to be a dream. If no one desired to have power over their neighbors, if no one feared their neighbors, if no one wished to have it all, what a wonderful place this would be.

This conflict of interest that mounts nation versus nation, religion versus religion, father versus son, it's all because of fear. Nations, like individuals, build great defense systems because they fear others. I have tremendous faith the time will come, probably not in our lifetimes, when we realize that there is nothing to fear. That is to say that the day will come when we as a people make a conscious decision to simply work together. For we all want one thing: peace. It all needs to start with the next generation. It will take time, no doubt, probably a few actual generations. But it will happen. I just know it.

As for me, one thing I haven't learned yet is how to play a guitar. I think it's time.

Credit: *Michael Dooley*

ABOUT THE AUTHOR

While Paul Martin lives in Boulder, Colorado, he travels throughout the world to participate in athletic events and throughout the United States to talk to groups of children and adults about dealing with adversities. Both his athletic event schedule and his speaking engagement schedule can be viewed at www.onemansleg.com